Praise for John Cisna
and
My McDonald's Diet

"I wish I had a teacher like you!"
— Matt Lauer, Host of NBC's *TODAY* show

"As a fitness professional who's seen nearly everything under the sun, I think John Cisna's experiment is nothing less than brilliant. The fact that he had his students track his results and learn about proper choices, discipline, the importance of balance, and the difference between good and bad calories is exactly what needs to be done. John has proven that a deconditioned person can become healthier by making a few wise choices each day. Bravo John — I'm a fan!"
— Clark Bartram, Author of *Where Your Mind Goes, You Go*

"In Iowa, a man said he's lost 40 pounds eating only McDonald's for three months. Not to be outdone, a man in Illinois lost 60 pounds after eating White Castle just once."
— Conan O'Brien, Host of TBS's *Conan*

*"Great book ... Just great!!!!!!!! And I say that not because you are my son-in-law. I say it because it is true. It is funny, insightful, inspiring, and above all a vehicle for the average person to say **I can do this!**"*
— Sharon Montgomery

"It's not the venue, it's the menu ... Leave it to a guy who ventured out on his own, to prove to himself and some students that life isn't dictated by those who say you can't. It's dictated by you ... saying you can."
— Neil Cavuto, Anchor and SVP, Fox News Channel

My McDonald's Diet
How I Lost 37 Pounds in 90 Days and Became a Viral Media Sensation

By John Cisna

with Ed Sweet

INSTINCT MEDIA LLC

Published in the United States of America by Instinct Media, LLC, Phoenix, Arizona. Contact Publisher@MyMcDonaldsDietBook.com

John Cisna is available for speaking engagements and educational presentations. To make arrangements, please write to John@MyMcDonaldsDietBook.com.

For free weight loss and other health tips, follow John Cisna on Twitter: @johncisna; on the Web: MyMcDonaldsDietBook.com; on Facebook: facebook.com/MyMcDonaldsDietBook.

ISBN: 9781632959843

Cover design by RJD Creative LLC
Cover photo by John Johnson

10 9 8 7 6 5 4 3 2 1

This book is dedicated to the students of Colo-NESCO Junior-Senior High School in Colo, Iowa. They're the reason I look forward to getting up each morning and going to school. They make me feel young again. I returned to teaching so I could make a difference, and it turns out that my students are the ones who've made a huge difference in my life. I'm blessed to work with such great kids in a great community.

My Relationship with McDonald's

Other than my interactions with the two McDonald's franchisees in Iowa who helped me facilitate my experiment, I had absolutely no contact with anyone from McDonald's before my story became national news. The McDonald's executives learned about my experiment when everyone else did.

Had McDonald's been involved in my project, I believe it would have tainted the outcome and would have prevented me from inspiring millions of people with the scientific proof that fast foods can be part of a healthy diet.

My experiment was in no way a PR stunt, and the attention it's received has surprised no one more than me. I believe that the project's authenticity is what made it resonate with people around the world.

Since the story of my experiment went viral, I have been in contact with people from McDonald's. I'm not sure what the future holds with them, if anything, but I do know that they were very cooperative with me while I wrote this book.

An Opportunity to Help Children

As a teacher, I know that our children hold the promise of a better future. So I'm donating a portion of the proceeds from every book I sell to Ronald McDonald House Charities. I'm proud to make this commitment so children with illness can have a fighting chance to make their own contributions to society. To learn more about this worthy cause, please take a moment out of your day to visit rmhc.org.

Note to Readers

Contents

Foreword by Neil Cavuto xi

Introduction 1
    Silence Is Golden 6
    Keeping the Peace 7
    The One Burning Question 8

Chapter 1: All in the Name of Science 10
    Oh Boy Are We Obese 10
    A Whale of a Tale 16

Chapter 2: A Few Fries Short of a Happy Meal 19
    Preconceived Notions 19
    The Girl of My Dreams 21

Chapter 3: Success and Discipline 23
    Cheaters Never Prosper 24
    Take Me Out to the Ballgame 24
    The Excitement Builds 27
    A Lesson from the Rat Race 28
    Teaching Outside the Box 29

Chapter 4: Choosing the Food, Glorious Food 33
    Balanced Days vs. Balanced Meals 34
    The Spice of Life 36
    A Fortunate Encounter 37
    The Good Ol' Boy Gang 40
    A Turkey of a Day 42

Chapter 5: Sweating it Out 45
    A Good Walk Spoiled 46
    Roaming the Halls 49

Chapter 6: The Results — Who's Laughing Now?............................51
    Becoming More "Desirable" 53
    Friends in Hy-Vee Places 55

Chapter 7: No Big Macs in the Big Apple 58
    Green Room Hunger Pangs 59
    Talking Baseball with Bob Costas 60
    Swooning over Kathie Lee 62
    All Hell Breaks Loose 63
    An Enemy at the Gate? 65
    Learning from My Mistakes 67
    A Radio Marathon 68
    Planes, Trains & Automobiles 69

Chapter 8: Going through a Phase — 2...73
    The Cisna Breakfast..74
    Move over, Arnold 74
    Phase 2 Sample Workouts 75
    What's Happening to Me? 78
    Streamlined Meal Plans..79
    Phase 2 Daily Menus..80
    Tears, Sweat and Blood 85

Chapter 9: What Choices Will You Make?.......................................87
    The Compound Effect...88
    A Diet Plan for Real People 89
    Patience Pays Off 91
    The Inspirational Wall..92

Epilogue..95

Acknowledgements..96

Bonus Section: My McDonald's Diet Daily Menus............................99

Foreword by Neil Cavuto

I remember a doctor telling me some years ago that there's no magic to losing weight. It's calories in, calories out. The idea is to burn off more calories than you take in. It's disarmingly simple, but to many Americans, including myself, impossibly difficult. Then along comes John Cisna, who takes even this simple advice and brings it to a whole new, yet tantalizing level. This isn't a new chapter in dieting. This is a whole new book. This book! It's like dieting's Holy Grail, served beneath, of all places, the Golden Arches!

When I first heard John's story — losing all this weight eating at McDonald's and only McDonald's — I was skeptical. How could that be? For one thing, the fast food police told me that could never be! Fast food was fast making us fat, and fat chance that would ever change, so how could it be responsible for making this one guy thin? Hadn't we learned from Morgan Spurlock in *Super Size Me* that McDonald's food didn't only make you fat, it made you sick? In Spurlock's case, his McDonald's-only diet not only made him gain 24 pounds, it sent his cholesterol level soaring to 230, and triggered horrible mood swings and sexual dysfunction as well!

I remember how the then 32-year-old film director's nauseating journey was hailed by the media as proof that fast food was no better than big tobacco in hooking us, fattening us and eventually killing us. Yet even then, the same media seemed to ignore that the Golden Arches was more than just big, old fat burgers. It offered other options, other choices. Fast food had them, but you'd be hard-pressed to find any in the media reporting them. Not so fair. Not so balanced. And along comes John Cisna to say, not so fast.

Leave it to Cisna to burst the burger bubble by reminding us those choices are even printed on a menu, the same menu as those Quarter-Pounder and Big Mac meals. Yogurt. Salads. Oatmeal. Egg White Delight McMuffins. They're all there. Pick and choose, or choose not to pick any at all. Our choice. Our call. Our … responsibility. I recall after having John on my show to discuss his weight loss, how Spurlock himself tweeted to take much of the credit; that John's success was made possible because of the very changes his earlier documentary inspired a decade ago.

No matter, the fact is that John Cisna lost nearly 40 pounds sticking to this fast food regimen, and that DOES matter, and that SHOULD matter.

It should matter to all of us who fight this battle of the bulge that we cannot make excuses that it's someone else's fault. We have choices in life. Gosh, fast food even offers us those choices in life. John made those choices, and varied those choices. But the bottom line, for his own waistline, is that McDonald's did provide those choices. Many of us, including myself, fail to take advantage of that, so we load up on the stuff that makes us fat. Obviously anyone dining on nothing but burgers and fries around the clock will soon be a lot more around the waist.

This is where common sense and John's remarkable discipline and simple charm kick in. He balanced things. Oatmeal and yogurt, salads and water. But he didn't do so at the total expense of other things — including cheeseburgers and fries. Never to excess. Always within reason. Each day. Every day. Exercising all days.

Calories in. Calories out. And throughout, John working it out. Day-by-day, eventually re-crafting a whole new body, that brings us to this day. John isn't only thinner. He shows us all how we can be, too. Not only thinner, but healthier and happier. He reminds us it's not the venue, it's the menu. He gets it. And he gets us. It "is" possible and John Cisna is the proof, and in this book, offers the proof. They say if something sounds too good to be true, it probably is. So listening to someone say he got thin eating nothing but McDonald's sounds like it's coming from a guy one fry short of a happy meal! But he's not. This book is not.

Food for thought. It's about focusing on what you eat.

Fat chance the media will ever grasp that. Leave it to a guy who ventured out on his own, to prove to himself and some students that life isn't dictated by those who say you can't. It's dictated by you … saying you can. That's the real skinny on John Cisna. That's the real skinny on losing weight. It's not about excuses and imaginary blocks. It's about personal discipline, and upending those blocks.

Neil Cavuto
Anchor and Senior Vice President
Fox News Channel
Fox Business Network

Introduction

"What's it like in Colo, Iowa?"
— Virtually every media personality I've met

On January 2, 2014 — at exactly 10:17 p.m. — my life changed forever. At that precise moment, I began a five-day, whirlwind transformation from simple science teacher in the small town of Colo, Iowa, to world-renowned media personality. It was a strange journey, to say the least.

That journey took me to the media capital of the world — New York City — where I was given the VIP treatment. I flew First Class. I rode around Manhattan in limousines. And I was welcomed into some of the biggest network and cable television studios on the planet. To put it mildly, I was thrust into a different kind of world than the one I'm used to in the outskirts of Des Moines. Around every corner was a person I recognized, respected and admired from watching TV. One minute I was shaking hands with Al Roker. The next I was talking baseball with Bob Costas. And then I found myself actually hugging Kathie Lee Gifford! These constant celebrity sightings literally gave me heart palpitations. And that was just before I had to go on the *TODAY* show with Matt Lauer and Savannah Guthrie and try to be witty, smart and articulate in front of an audience of about six million Americans, give or take a few.

You may have seen me on the *TODAY* show, *Good Morning America*, *Fox & Friends* or *Your World with Neil Cavuto*. By the end of January 7, 2014, my face had been seen on television by an estimated 14 million Americans from coast to coast and on the Internet by many millions more worldwide. My story was number one on *Yahoo! News*. Thanks to doing scores of radio interviews, my voice was heard across the country, as well as in world capitals like Dublin, Warsaw and Sydney. And my story has been featured in too many newspapers and magazines to count, including

USA TODAY and *Time* in the U.S. and *The Daily Mail* and *Metro News* overseas. Heck, I was even the butt of a joke in one of Conan O'Brien's monologues.

All this attention — just for eating at McDonald's!

Dining under the Golden Arches is something that nearly 70 million of us do every single day, and I've been singled out for it. Like Morgan Spurlock, the writer and director of the documentary *Super Size Me*, eating at McDonald's is something that will define me for the rest of my days. Don't get me wrong — I embrace this reality with great enthusiasm. In fact, eating nothing but McDonald's for breakfast, lunch and dinner for three months probably saved my life. But never in a million years would I have thought that my crazy little McDonald's Diet experiment would attract such massive amounts of interest around the world.

During my TODAY show appearance, Matt Lauer said he wished he had a teacher like me! With Savannah Guthrie (left) and Joy Bauer.

On the night when my life changed forever, I was playing cards with some buddies of mine like I do every other week. The only thing different about this particular card game was that I knew I was going to be featured on KCCI, the CBS affiliate out of Des Moines. Earlier that day, reporter Mark Tauscheck and his camera crew spent a few hours with me at the school where I teach. My friends and I planned to watch the segment, have a good laugh at my expense and then go back to playing cards.

We stopped our game at 10:00 p.m. to turn on the news, and my story came on at exactly 10:17 p.m. I really liked how they flipped my before-and-after pictures, so it looked like I had really gained tons of weight during my experiment. But the big surprise for the audience in the Des Moines metropolitan area was that this local boy actually *lost* all that weight from consuming all that McDonald's food. The reporter described my story as a reverse *Super Size Me*, proving to the world that losing weight is less about where you eat than it is about making smart choices.

Naturally, my buddies ribbed me about the segment when it was over and about 30 seconds later I got a call from Brandon Kelley, the principal of Colo-NESCO Junior-Senior High School.

"Oh my God, Cisna!" my boss yelled at the top of his lungs.

I swallowed hard, not knowing where this was going.

"Couldn't you have at least put a shirt on?!"

We shared a big belly laugh over my before-and-after pictures being broadcast to tens, if not hundreds, of thousands of people throughout the Hawkeye State. We both agreed that the piece was pretty neat, and that it was cool to get a little exposure for my high school. Then I went back to my card game, assuming that I could get back to my regular life now that my 15 minutes of fame were over.

Well, things didn't exactly work out that way. It didn't take long for my phone to start ringing again. I heard from family members and friends, some of whom I hadn't spoken with in years. And I got other calls, which were even more unexpected. The country's major news organizations were trying to find me. The first one to track me down was ABC's *Good Morning America*. They talked to me two days after the segment aired on KCCI, and that was the start of the avalanche.

On Sunday, January 5, a few hours after the *Good Morning America* segment aired, I got a call from my daughter Jamie. She was out of breath, saying something about people from New York wanting to talk to me.

"They said they're from the *TODAY* show!" she said excitedly. "Dad, what's going on?"

"How in the world did they get your phone number?" I asked, trying to stay calm.

"I don't know!" she yelled. "What do they want?"

"I don't have a clue, Jamie," I replied. "But what was that number again?"

As soon as I hung up with my daughter, I called the number and found myself speaking to a very pleasant woman who identified herself as one of the producers of the *TODAY* show. She told me that she had seen the piece on KCCI, as well as my *Good Morning America* segment.

"We'd like to fly you to New York and have you on the *TODAY* show tomorrow," she said.

I'm not usually at a loss for words, but at that moment I couldn't put a sentence together if my life depended on it. Realizing that mama didn't raise no dummy, I managed to blurt out, "Sure, I think I can do that." I didn't even know what my schedule called for at school the next day!

"Great!" said the producer, perkily. She told me that she was going to check on the travel and call me back soon.

I hung up the phone and bounded up the stairs, squealing like a little Iowa greased pig. "Kim!" I screamed to my wife. "You're not going to believe the phone call I just had!"

I explained everything that had just happened, while Kim sat there listening to me in total disbelief. "What are you going to do?" she asked.

"I'm going to wait by the phone!"

About 20 minutes later, the producer called me back. "The last available flight leaves Des Moines in two and a half hours," she said. "Is there any way you can get on it?"

"That shouldn't be a problem," I said. "I can pack a suitcase and leave in about an hour."

I detected some nervousness in the producer's voice when she asked if that was going to give me enough time. I realized she didn't quite understand that getting on a flight at the Des Moines International Airport didn't involve the same kind of *Indiana Jones*-like adventure you have to go through at any of the New York airports. "Oh, I'll be on that flight, alright," I said, trying not to laugh.

The excitement level was off the charts at the Cisna house as I scrambled to pack my bag for my stint as a guest on the *TODAY* show. My wife was giving me advice about how to handle myself with Matt Lauer, while I was trying to find clean underwear and a matching pair of socks.

As I was finally getting into the car to head to the airport, my phone rang again. This time, it was my oldest daughter, Dani, telling me that some people from Fox News in New York were trying to reach me. It was déjà vu all over again — only 45 minutes later!

"Dad, what's going on?" Dani asked.

"I don't have a clue," I replied, just as I did to my younger daughter. "But what was that number again?"

I called Fox News immediately and spoke with another pleasant-sounding young producer. She said that they wanted to book me for a satellite interview on *Fox & Friends*, the morning show on the Fox News Channel.

"I have a better idea," I said. I let her know that I was going to be in New York anyway, appearing on the *TODAY* show. "If you're willing to pay for my hotel tomorrow night, I could do the interview live on Tuesday morning."

"No problem," she said. "Where will you be staying?"

I realized that I never got that information from the *TODAY* show folks, so I told the Fox producer that I'd have to call her back. And, as I was hanging up the phone, it dawned on me that I still hadn't called my boss! By the time I got near the airport, I spoke with Principal Kelley, got all the logistics of my trip figured out and was able to finally start thinking about what was actually happening to me.

As I drove into the airport and saw the planes coming in and taking off to various destinations, I realized that this burger-eating Iowa boy was heading into the media center of the world with no direction, no plan and no idea where all this was going. In the following pages, I'll tell you all about my adventures and what it's been like being a viral media sensation.

Silence Is Golden

When I got home from New York, I took the first opportunity I could to lock myself in my home office, sit in complete silence and try to figure out what I had just been through. It was obvious that people were interested in my story, and clearly, my life was never going to be the same.

I've had thousands of requests for my McDonald's Diet menus. People want to know how I lost so much weight, even though I ate nothing but breakfast, lunch and dinner at McDonald's for 90 days. And people want to know what it was like, from the inside out, to be suddenly thrust into the national spotlight.

So that's what I've set out to accomplish in this book. If you're interested in losing weight, I hope I can give you a new perspective on dieting, along with some valuable tools you can use to take off the pounds and keep them off — by eating at McDonald's or anywhere else you want to eat. I'll explain my entire 90-day regimen, and give you the daily menus my students developed for me during the three-month experiment.

You can skip to the end of this book to get all the diet details, but I hope you'll take the time to read everything else related to the experiment we conducted. You'll learn about the key nutrients we tracked, how moderate exercise fits into a successful weight-loss program and how responsible choices can not only improve your health, but also enhance virtually every other aspect of your life.

If you just want to know what it's like to live in a fishbowl, you'll find it here, too. Hopefully, I'll entertain you with anecdotes from my adventures in New York, like the time I looked over at the makeup chair next to mine and saw my hero Bob Costas; how no one believed I wanted to keep eating McDonald's when there were so many great restaurants around; and which media personality surprised me by taking the time to write me a personal thank-you note.

In addition to witty stories and factual information about nutrition and exercise, I'll also share my personal perceptions of the whole experience. You'll find out what it means to me to be a teacher. You'll learn how I lived through Thanksgiving while my family gorged themselves on turkey with all the trimmings. And you'll get my advice for dealing with people who think whatever it is you're doing is absolutely ridiculous.

If nothing else, I hope my story inspires you to go for your dreams and desires, despite what other people may think. In all honesty, I have to say that even if I didn't become an overnight sensation from eating at McDonald's, and if the students, parents, teachers and administrators of Colo-NESCO Junior-Senior High School still had reason to laugh at me today, I wouldn't have done anything differently.

Keeping the Peace

Throughout my entire adult life, I've tried to take great comfort in the Serenity Prayer, written by the American theologian Reinhold Niebuhr and popularized by Alcoholics Anonymous and other twelve-step programs. You may know it in its shortened form, but I like the original, longer version best:

God, give me grace to accept with serenity
The things that cannot be changed,
Courage to change the things
Which should be changed,
And the Wisdom to distinguish
The one from the other.

Living one day at a time,
Enjoying one moment at a time,
Accepting hardship as a pathway to peace,

Taking, as Jesus did,
This sinful world as it is,
Not as I would have it,
Trusting that You will make all things right,
If I surrender to Your will,
So that I may be reasonably happy in this life,
And supremely happy with You forever in the next.

Amen.

Whether you believe in God or not, these are truly valuable words to live by. They've certainly helped me get through all kinds of challenges and adversity, and I expect to rely on them on many more occasions in the future.

The One Burning Question

Now, before I get into my story, I'd like to answer the one question I was asked more than any other during the media frenzy that was my life for a week or so: "What's it like in Colo, Iowa?"

Colo is a perfect example of a small, Midwestern town with old-fashioned values. I'm willing to bet that you won't ever meet a group of finer, nicer or friendlier people in the world than the people who live and work in Colo.

The high school where I teach, Colo-NESCO Junior-Senior High School, is a small school by Iowa standards. Only 184 students roam the halls. Everyone knows each other. And the community is very close. When I was in the business world, every organization I was ever a part of had at least one bad apple, but that's absolutely not the case at this special school. All of us teachers get along well with each other. We go to Buffalo Wild Wings after parent-teacher conferences and volunteer as much as we can to help out with extracurricular activities. I can honestly say that my colleagues have been the best people to spend 40 to 60 hours a week with.

I feel blessed to be so welcome in this community, especially since no one else seemed to want a teacher who was returning to the profession at an age when most people were leaving it. Despite the fact that I was certified in biology, chemistry, physics, physical science, general science and junior-high mathematics — and had a rare and valuable coaching endorsement to boot — I had a tough time finding a job anywhere at age 50.

Then came Colo-NESCO Junior-Senior High School. When small schools get an opportunity to hire someone in the science and math fields, with as many certifications as I have, it's like a gift from heaven. Because I was qualified to teach a variety of different classes, the district was able to assign me multiple preps, or subjects, and have me coach a few different teams. In my two years in the Colo-NESCO district, I've taught seventh-grade life science, eighth-grade earth science, eighth-grade math, 10th-grade biology, high-school physics and high-school chemistry. I'm also an assistant football coach and head girls' golf coach. Six different preps and two coaching gigs is a lot for a single teacher in most school districts, but not at Colo-NESCO.

Neither my colleagues nor I mind working hard to help our students become the very best they can be. Motivating young people is incredibly challenging, but when you can reach a student and make a difference in his or her life, the feeling of joy you experience is immeasurable. It's in that spirit that I offer this book to you. I hope that in some small way I can make a difference in your life, and I hope you'll let me know about it if I do.

Chapter 1: All in the Name of Science

"Suddenly I had a whole new way to think about food."
— Vicki Cobb, *Science Experiments You Can Eat: Revised Edition*

At the start of every school year, I ask my sophomore biology students to begin thinking about their big semester project. They get to choose the subject matter, because if they pick something they're interested in they have a better chance of taking their learning to the next level. The project can be about anything they want, as long as it's related to biology.

Once they select a topic, my students must create a hypothesis and set up an experiment that will either prove the hypothesis to be true or show it to be false. In the past, students have investigated the effects of different amounts of sunlight on growing plants; the efficiency of microwave popcorn brands at different price points; how knuckle-popping correlates to enlarged joints; and whether or not you can teach an old dog new tricks. (It turns out, you can!)

Before the 2013–2014 school year started, I had an opportunity to have dinner with a man named Kevin O'Brien. He was dating my wife's best friend, and it turned out that he owns several McDonald's franchises in the area. We got to talking over dinner one night, and it occurred to me that some of my students might get a kick out of seeing if someone could actually get healthy eating at McDonald's. It would be an interesting semester project.

Oh Boy Are We Obese

I knew that obesity was a huge problem in America. According to the Centers for Disease Control and Prevention (CDC), more than one-third of American adults

(35.7%) are obese today. If you add in the number of men and women who are "just" overweight, the number jumps to more than two-thirds of the country (69.2%)!

We all know the damaging effects of this. Today, obesity has the dubious honor of being the second-leading cause of preventable death in America. Carrying extra weight around increases our risk for a number of negative health conditions, including type 2 diabetes, high blood pressure and heart disease. Because of this, the CDC estimates that the annual medical costs for obese people are nearly $1,500 higher than those for people of normal weight.

Many people blame McDonald's and other fast food restaurants for the country's obesity epidemic. They believe that there's a connection because Americans started getting fatter late in the twentieth century — around the same time that fast food chains proliferated. Films like *Super Size Me* play into the perception that fast food companies are the villains, duping innocent souls into becoming uncontrollable, calorie-consuming addicts.

I never fully bought into the myth that burger joints were ruining the country. As a scientist I thought *Super Size Me* was irresponsible journalism, and it frustrated me when I heard about teachers showing that movie in classes that deal with health or nutrition. Of course someone who purposely eats 5,000 calories a day with no exercise is going to gain weight. What's the big surprise there? More astonishing to me was the revelation that "Big Mac Enthusiast" Don Gorske — who appears in the film eating his 19,000th sandwich — manages to keep his cholesterol at 140 and his weight in check despite the fact that 90 percent of his solid-food diet is comprised of Big Macs!

Filmmaker Morgan Spurlock does include Jared Fogle in *Super Size Me* — and even credits the Subway spokesman for inspiring people with his "will power and giant pants" — but the film goes to extremes to bash the fast food industry in general and McDonald's in particular. Spurlock claims that there are people out there who eat like he did in his 30-day experiment, but he doesn't have any real data to support it. The movie may be entertaining, but it really isn't very good science.

Thinking that I might be able to call the link between fast food and obesity into question, especially since more healthy options can be found on the McDonald's menu than when *Super Size Me* was filmed and released in 2003–2004, I decided to do what Spurlock did in reverse. Instead of taking an in-shape person and gorging him so his liver malfunctions, I thought it would be interesting to see if an out-of-shape person could get healthier by eating nothing but breakfast, lunch and dinner at McDonald's. And I wanted to back up my experiment with as much hard data as I could collect.

At the beginning of the school year, I asked my students if any of them were interested in going into the medical or nutrition field in some way. Three kids, Tanner Clatt, Savannah Deupree and Grant Tiarks raised their hands. I approached these three kids after class and told them about my McDonald's Diet idea. I asked them if they wanted to make it their semester project, and they all agreed.

Naturally, I offered myself up as the guinea pig. In addition to the obvious liability factors involved in asking for a student volunteer, I don't think it would have gone over too well if I told some parents that I wanted to use their fat son for an experiment that required him to eat nothing but McDonald's for 90 days. I would have been fired and run out of town in about two minutes.

Plus, I certainly fit the bill as the quintessential out-of-shape subject. My starting weight when the experiment began on September 16, 2013, was a whopping 280.2 pounds. My body mass index (BMI) was 38 — eight points above the number that's considered obese. My chest measured 48.5 inches, my hips were 49 inches and my stomach stretched the tape to 51 inches. Any man whose waist is over 40 inches is at a higher risk of getting heart disease and type 2 diabetes — and I was 11 inches more than that! It sure was a far cry from my baseball days at Iowa State, when I weighed a svelte 185 pounds and could do the 60-yard dash in 6.6 seconds — in spikes!

In college my metabolism was on fire. I could eat anything I wanted and stay a fit 185 pounds as an outfielder for the Iowa State Cyclones.

With the students signed on to help run the experiment, and their subject ready to take his first bite out of a Quarter Pounder with Cheese, we got to work. I gave the kids two parameters they had to follow. Number one, they had to keep me as close as they could to a total of 2,000 calories a day. That's the number of daily calories all those Nutrition Facts labels are based on, and it's also the calorie intake that most weight-loss programs, such as Jenny Craig and Weight Watchers, use for adults.

The second thing my students had to do was create daily menus for me that stayed within 100 percent of the recommended dietary allowances (RDA) of the 15 different nutritional values we were tracking. This became a balancing act for the kids. Coming up with daily menus that totaled 2,000 calories was pretty easy, but my students had to use a lot more scrutiny to make sure they had all the nutrients in the right proportion.

Three of my sophomore biology students — Tanner Clatt (left), Grant Tiarks and Savannah Deupree — worked with me on the project and were responsible for making my daily menus.

The work involved in creating the menus was the least favorite part of the experiment for the kids, but, in my opinion, it's what truly made it a valuable learning experience for them. Tanner, Savannah and Grant were forced to develop their critical-thinking skills in order to make necessary adjustments as the experiment progressed. For example, just a few days into the project the students realized that they had to remove orange juice and Egg McMuffins from my diet to get our numbers for sugar and cholesterol under control.

As you can see from Figure 1, the kids did a pretty good job hitting our targets with the food items they had to work with. On average, we were right where we needed to be with our total calories, fat calories, total fat, saturated fat, carbs, dietary fiber, sugar and calcium. We were above our target in sodium, protein, vitamin A and vitamin C, and below our target in iron. My trans fats were way off because most restaurants — including McDonald's — have removed them from their cooking processes. In hindsight, that was one category we probably didn't even need to track.

Fig. 1

Nutritional Values	Avg. Percent of RDA
1. Total Calories	94.12%
2. Fat Calories	92.21%
3. Total Fat	93.56%
4. Saturated Fat	99.22%
5. Trans Fat	.09%
6. Cholesterol	72.31%
7. Sodium	166.16%
8. Total Carbs	83.83%
9. Dietary Fiber	104.83%
10. Sugar	105.12%
11. Protein	167.49%
12. Vitamin A	204.09%
13. Vitamin C	385.42%
14. Calcium	113.34%
15. Iron	63.19%

At no time did I think I was in any jeopardy from nutrient levels that didn't come as close to the RDA as we wanted. In fact, I was happy to be consuming more vitamin C during the fall and winter months, and the extra protein was a plus because we decided to integrate exercise into the program.

I was criticized on national television for eating too much salt as part of my McDonald's Diet. Figure 1 shows that I was consuming an average of about 1-2/3 times the current RDA, which is 2,300 mg. However, many dietitians are recommending a nearly two-fold increase in the RDA for sodium in healthy individuals, because the link between excess sodium and health problems is proving to be a tenuous one at best. On July 8, 2011, *Scientific American* ran a great piece by Melinda Wenner Moyer titled "It's Time to End the War on Salt." The article reported on studies that found "no strong evidence that cutting salt intake reduces the risk for heart attacks, strokes or death in people with normal or high blood pressure," and it made a compelling case for calling off the salt police.

A Whale of a Tale

With our methodology in place, I took my measurements — and my infamous "before" picture. As I said to *TODAY's* Savannah Guthrie and Matt Lauer, "If I had gotten any bigger, I'd probably have to avoid harpoons!" When I stepped on the scale to get my initial reading, a ticket popped out that said, "One at a time, please!" And when I discovered that my stomach was 51 inches in diameter, I was in such shock that I had to run to the refrigerator to get a sandwich!

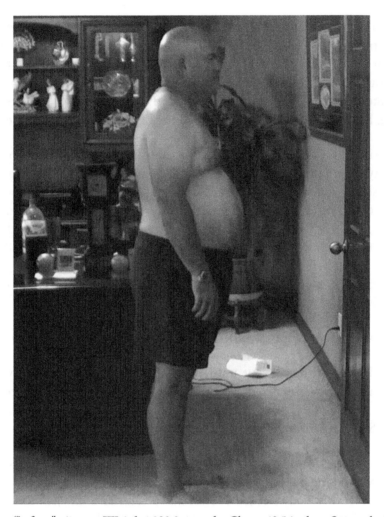

My infamous "before" picture: Weight: 280.2 pounds; Chest: 48.5 inches; Stomach: 51 inches; Hips: 49 inches

Like other athletes who compete at the college level, I gave up sports when I realized baseball would never be my career. In my case, a severe shoulder injury ruined any chance I had of becoming a Major League ballplayer. Quite honestly, exercise was never something I did for fun, or for my health. For me, being in shape was really just a side effect of pursuing excellence in baseball. When that pursuit ended, I stopped training and started gaining.

In fact, I've battled weight all my life. In my younger days, it was never a big deal for me to put on 15 or 20 pounds from time to time. My metabolism was high enough that I could easily take off any unwanted weight when I needed to in a matter of weeks. But as I got older, my metabolism slowed down. I'd occasionally resort to a program like Jenny Craig to take the weight off. I'd be down to a reasonable weight for a while, but then I'd eventually gain it all back again — and then some!

By the time I hit age 50, it was over. And for the past five years now, I've never weighed any less than 260 pounds. Believe it or not, the thing that really did me in was the baseball coaching I do in the summer for Ballard High School in Huxley, Iowa. How could you possibly gain weight when you're out on the field for up to 10 hours a day, you ask? Easy. I'd grab a burger here and there, and by the time I got home at 10:00 or 10:30 p.m. I'd be famished. I'd consume 2,000 to 3,000 calories in one sitting right before going to bed, and it would usually be in the form of anything I could get my hands on as quickly as possible — including chips, candy, cookies and pizza.

There I was, super sizing myself!

I knew I was getting fat, but until I saw the before picture for my McDonald's Diet experiment I never realized how much I had really ballooned. Once that picture was taken, I couldn't deny the fact that I was a big fatty. If there was ever a time that I needed the Serenity Prayer, it was then!

I had Niebuhr's words to calm me down, but I also knew that I had science on my side. When you do the math, there was no possible way I could've gained weight on my McDonald's Diet. My body needed at least 2,500 calories a day just to maintain itself, and I was restricting my caloric intake to 2,000 a day. With a 20 percent calorie deficit, my body had no choice but to draw from the massive stores of fat I had accumulated over the years to give me energy. However, as you'll see in the next chapter, I couldn't find anyone who thought I'd be able to lose weight in this experiment.

Chapter 2: A Few Fries Short of a Happy Meal

"Only Cisna would come up with something as ridiculous as this."
— Josh Nessa, head football coach and social studies teacher,
Colo-NESCO Junior-Senior High School

When word got out about my little experiment, people weren't shy about telling me what they thought of it. Consensus around campus was that I was basically out of my mind, off my rocker and about as dumb as a box of rocks for coming up with this so-called diet, which was doomed to failure before it even started.

Obviously, these people weren't familiar with the scientific method. When you set out to prove or disprove a hypothesis, there really isn't any success or failure — just a result, backed up by data.

Granted, there was also a personal element at play. I wanted to "succeed," if that meant losing weight. And, like I said, the experiment really was "rigged" to work. What shocked and amused me was that people let their feelings about McDonald's get in the way of the facts.

Preconceived Notions

"McDonald's is really unhealthy," commented one student as we roamed the hallways with a video camera, asking kids what they thought of the project.

"It doesn't matter how much you walk, I still think you'd get fat," said another.

One boy said I was "an idiot," another girl predicted that I'd gain "at least" 100 pounds, and another student called the experiment "a complete waste of time."

"Absolutely impossible!" exclaimed one student, when asked if a person could get healthier by eating nothing but McDonald's for breakfast, lunch and dinner for 90 straight days. Another girl asked if this was some kind of a trick question!

The vast majority of other student responses were similarly negative. It seemed that the student body of Colo-NESCO Junior-Senior High School thought I had a better chance of growing hair on my head than getting healthy by eating at McDonald's!

I didn't fare too much better with the adults on campus, although perhaps they were slightly more charitable.

English teacher Priscilla Gammons thought I was "crazy." Dana Accola, who teaches family consumer science, believed that the experiment would be "an interesting test of will power." And Jackie Dunlap, the school nurse, was "very skeptical." Only one person, social studies teacher and head football coach Josh Nessa, thought that I could actually lose weight on my diet, but he didn't think I'd lose very much.

All of these people were in good company. In the movie *Super Size Me*, 95 out of 100 nutritionists interviewed agreed that fast food is "a major contributor to the obesity epidemic sweeping America." Forty-five of these nutritionists said that you should never eat fast food. Twenty-eight of them thought you could get away with a fast food meal somewhere between once a week and once or twice per month. And only two of the nutritionists surveyed thought that it was okay to eat fast food twice a week or more.

When it came to my family, I got mixed reactions. My sister-in-law, who just happens to be a registered dietitian, looked at me as if I had a carrot growing out of my forehead. And my daughter Dani went completely ballistic. "That's so stupid!" she screamed, starting to cry. "You're going to kill yourself!"

Dani was so inconsolable that I thought I was going to have to restrain her with Houdini's straitjacket. In order to calm her down, I had to promise her that I'd stop the experiment halfway through if my blood work came back negative.

In contrast, my other two daughters thought the whole thing was kind of cool. They weren't sure what the results would be, but I guess they trusted me not to do something to hurt myself intentionally. Or maybe they just wouldn't be as upset as their sister would be if something really bad happened to their dear old dad!

The Girl of My Dreams

I received the most support from my wife, Kim. After 37 years together, she's used to my impulsive antics and outlandish schemes. Compared to some of the other things I've sprung on her, this McDonald's Diet experiment was a piece of cake.

I have to say, if anyone has a direct path to heaven, it's Kim. She's always been there for me when I needed her most. We were the proverbial high-school sweethearts, and we got married when I was just a sophomore in college. We're complete opposites in many ways, and we disagree on pretty much everything from politics and religion to fashion and shopping. We try hard to respect each other and learn from each other's point of view, and I think that's why we've been able to stay together for so long and remain best friends. I'm sure I speak for a lot of guys when I say how lucky I am to get my true strength from my wife.

Five years ago, at age 50, I made what was probably the biggest decision of my life — to leave a high-paying job to become a teacher again. Despite my strong connection with Kim, I was scared to death about asking for her blessing.

I sat down with her one night and simply told her that I didn't want to be in the rat race anymore.

"What do you want to do?" she asked, without even a hint of anxiety.

"I want to go were my heart's always been," I replied. "I want go back into teaching and coaching."

"Let's do it," she said, not letting on that she was freaking out, which she would have had every right to do.

I was the luckiest man in the world. It was such a relief to get her support, and that made me work even harder to achieve my dream. There was no way I was going to let her down.

We swallowed hard, refinanced our house and used my 401(k) to get ready for my return to teaching. For about a year I had no retirement fund, and I was facing a house payment that I knew would be a challenge on a teacher's salary.

After going through a huge life change like that, my announcement that I was going to eat nothing but McDonald's for three months didn't faze Kim at all. In fact, because she knew how persistent and stubborn I could be, I think she believed that I might actually lose a few pounds! In the back of her mind I think she imagined me slimming down to the weight I was when we first fell in love. I guess she really didn't like me being twice the man I used to be!

While pretty much everyone thought I was a few fries short of a Happy Meal, the woman I love stood by my side. And that was more important to me than anything else in the world.

Chapter 3: Success and Discipline

"All great truths begin as blasphemies."
— George Bernard Shaw, *Annajanska the Bolshevik Empress*

I'm no revolutionary, but I took comfort in the fact that so many of the great scientific figures throughout history — from Galileo to the Wright Brothers to "Crazy Fritz" Zwicky (who discovered dark matter) — had more than their fair share of doubters and naysayers. The fact that most of the people around me didn't believe that I'd lose weight by eating nothing but McDonald's for breakfast, lunch and dinner for 90 days made me want to do it even more.

I've lived my whole life trying not to be influenced by what other people think. When all is said and done, the only things that really matter to me are myself, my family and my closest friends. If I can't change it, I don't worry about it. That's my shortened version of the Serenity Prayer.

Intellectually, I knew that the only thing keeping me from losing weight during this experiment was my will power. If I didn't cheat or give up, it would be physically impossible for me to either gain weight or even stay the same weight that I was. Without a doubt, my "after" picture was going to be much more beautiful than my before picture! By the end of the 90 days, it would certainly *look* like my students and I had proved our hypothesis. Even though the real validation would be in the blood work, nobody would even care about that if I weren't considerably thinner in three months' time.

The only thing stopping me from losing weight on my McDonald's Diet would be me. I had single-handedly *prevented* my own weight loss for decades by making poor food choices, working too much and taking exercise out of my life, so why couldn't I do the exact opposite? There were only three people to blame for my 280 pounds— me, myself and I! The fast food industry wasn't brainwashing me to get fat, like the film *Super Size Me* wants us all to believe. I'm ultimately responsible for how thin or fat I am at any given time, and I was surprised by how quickly the people around me were willing to vilify "Big Burger." I guess it's just easier for us to blame a faceless corporation for an obesity epidemic than it is to blame ourselves.

All I had to do to lose my fat was change my behavior and stick to the plan. Thank goodness for the hecklers around me, because they gave me the motivation I needed to stay focused and prove them wrong.

Cheaters Never Prosper

Most diets set people up for failure, and my McDonald's Diet was no exception. I was limiting my calories far below what I normally consumed in a day as a certified foodaholic, and I was doing it cold turkey. I went from consuming whole pizzas with extra breadsticks; two or three bowls of sugary cereal; whole bags of kettle chips; and 22-oz. rib-eye steaks with all the trimmings — easily 4,000 to 5,000 calories a day — to having only 2,000 daily calories for 90 days straight.

It's a fact that most people cheat on their diets. So much cheating goes on that most diet programs these days even encourage building in a once-a-week cheat day! The idea is that anyone can handle a restricted diet for a short period of time, but not for the long haul. Without structured cheating, so the theory goes, the pent up frustration of being on a diet can lead to outright binges. Cheat days — where taboo foods are allowed and calorie counts be damned — take some of the pressure off.

I had no such advantage during my three-month experiment, although some people might argue that I was cheating all the time since I got to eat McDonald's every day! True, I may have had my share of Quarter Pounders and sundaes, but I never exceeded the number of calories dictated by my daily menus.

Take Me Out to the Ballgame

As I've already mentioned, having so many people think that I wasn't going to make it really got my competitive juices flowing. Now, I'm no psychologist, and I don't really know what makes one person give up their commitments and another follow through with them, but I do know that my love of baseball helped fuel my competitive drive and my hunger to succeed at what I do.

When I was young, my father, John Sr., encouraged me to play sports and be the best I could be. He was an outstanding athlete in high school and college, and became friends with a lot of great athletes who made names for themselves while he pursued a career as a doctor.

My father loved me and exposed me to a lot of great experiences, but he didn't let me get away with much. I grew up on the tough east side of Des Moines, and my father did everything he could to make me more resilient when things didn't go my way. It may have caused me some pain at the time, but in the long run it helped me handle adversity and the inherent unfairness of life.

He used this same philosophy when he taught me how to hit a baseball. In my very first Little League game, it was obvious that I was afraid of the pitcher. Every time a pitch would come in, I'd step away from the plate. To fix this problem, my dad took me out behind the barn next to our property for hitting practice. He threw dozens, if not hundreds, of pitches at me, constantly telling me to turn into the ball instead of bailing out of the way. "I don't care how close they are," he said. "Turn into them!"

About 110 percent of his pitches hit me along the right side of my body. Fortunately, he never hit my head! "Now that didn't hurt, did it?" he'd ask, after each ball made its stinging impact on my tender skin.

It hurt like hell, but I knew it would hurt a lot more if I didn't tell my dad what he wanted to hear. "No dad," I replied each time. "It didn't hurt!"

We finally got done with my "lesson" when my dad's arm got too tired to throw anymore and it got too dark to see. That night, my mother happened to notice all the welts along my entire right side.

"How in the world did you get those?" she asked anxiously.

"Oh, Dad threw baseballs at me," I replied.

You should've heard the "conversation" between my mother and father that night! My father never threw another baseball at me again, and I never stepped away from the plate, either.

In fact, I became quite a good player. My love for baseball really blossomed when my father graduated from medical school and became the team physician for a Triple-A baseball club in Des Moines called the Iowa Oaks. He had set up his own practice as an Ob/Gyn, and basically offered general medical services to the team in return for season tickets to every home game. I spent all my summers from age 8 to 14 at Sec Taylor Stadium, rubbing elbows with a Who's Who of Major League players-to-be. Joe Rudi honed his skills on the Oaks, and so did Gene Tenace, Marcel and Rene Lachemann, Vida Blue, José Morales, Joe Carter and a young unknown second baseman named Tony La Russa. My dad got really close with these guys, delivering their babies and watching them move on to the Major Leagues. To this day, my dad and José Morales are like brothers.

Being around such incredible talent inspired me to work hard on my own baseball skills. I got good enough to make the Senior League All-Star team when I was just 13. I passed on that opportunity to play varsity ball as a freshman at Johnston High School. In my senior year, we won the state championship as the only team to ever go undefeated in our conference. That year I also played in the state's very first All-Star series for high school players and was voted MVP.

After high school I attended Southwestern Junior College in Creston, Iowa. I did very well on the baseball team, hitting just shy of .400 in my first season. The summer after freshman year, José Morales invited me to come up and spend a week with him while he was playing for the Minnesota Twins. I found out very quickly why he ended up being one of the greatest pinch hitters in the history of the game: his work ethic was second to none. We went to the ballpark each day about an hour before any of his teammates were required to be there. We'd go to the outfield batting cages and throw each other batting practice. I found out that he did this same routine every single day, and I believe it was the primary reason he was able to have such a long career in the Major Leagues.

That same summer, I went to a Cincinnati Reds tryout camp. At these camps, they separate all the guys by position and time each group in the 60-yard dash. I easily won my race against all the other first basemen, which qualified me for another race against all the other position winners. I beat everyone in the final race, too, which got the attention of the head coach of Iowa State. I didn't even know he was there! A week before I was supposed to go back to Southwestern Junior College,

Iowa State's head coach contacted me and said that he wanted me to come play for him. He even offered a full tuition and books scholarship to entice me.

Knowing that I was a good hitter and could run like the wind, the coaches at Iowa State moved me to the outfield. The problem was that I just couldn't throw. For some reason, I couldn't get any snap on the ball. It turned out that I had a big lump of calcium in my rotator cuff, apparently from an old shoulder dislocation I didn't even know had ever happened!

Unfortunately, as I mentioned earlier, a pretty major surgery on that shoulder during my junior year of college put a quick end to my dreams of playing professional baseball. I was fine with that and was very thankful that my abilities at least gave me a good college education. And besides, I was a newlywed with different priorities than most guys who wanted to play baseball for a living.

The Excitement Builds

At the beginning of my McDonald's Diet everyone started to get excited, including myself. It was kind of fun being the center of attention, even if a lot of that attention was critical. Don't misunderstand: there wasn't any malice against me. Most, if not all, of the criticism was good-natured. And like I said before, the skepticism was actually a good thing because it fueled my competitive spirit when my stomach started grumbling for more food.

But that wasn't the only thing that motivated me to stay on my McDonald's Diet for the full 90 days. Primary among them was my infamous before picture, which I put on the desktop of my computer to constantly remind me how far I had let myself go. Seeing that picture every day scared me to death and made it easier for me to resist any temptation to stray from the very specific menus my students were planning for me.

My sense of responsibility was also a huge motivator. The owner of the McDonald's restaurant in Nevada, Iowa, where I got my food for the experiment, agreed to provide my meals at no cost to me. The total bill came close to $2,000! I wasn't about to let down the people who stuck their necks out on an idea that wasn't even theirs. And remember, Kevin O'Brien, the McDonald's franchisee who helped make this whole thing happen, was going out with my wife's best friend. If I messed up, Kim would have killed me!

A Lesson from the Rat Race

When all was said and done, I had total control over the experiment. It was my idea. I made the rules. And I didn't have to rely on anyone under me to get results, like I did when I was a salesperson.

For the last 10 years of my business career, I was the Midwest regional sales director and the director of training for a well-known telecommunications company. In those 10 years I made a lot of money and consistently performed well enough to take my wife on some pretty nice trips to different parts of the world. These company "President's Club" trips were reserved for the top five percent of producers, and they included exciting adventures in Cancun, an exploration of the California wine country and a fabulous 10-day Mediterranean cruise that set sail from Barcelona.

A lot of people don't realize that a high level of personal stress often accompanies financial success. Although I did very well in my capacity as a sales executive, I started to realize that the pressure to constantly meet or exceed my targets was going to drive me to an early grave.

My boss during this time remains one of the best men I've ever been associated with. I didn't always agree with his management style, but he helped me realize one of the most important lessons I've ever learned: to be truly successful you have to look for the path to accomplish your goals, rather than focus on reasons why you can't attain them. It seems like such a simple thing, but it's incredibly hard to put into practice. It's so much easier to think that the cards are stacked against you and to blame others for your failures. It's just like people blaming McDonald's for making them fat.

After 25 years in the business world, I realized that I had been spending a lot of time convincing myself why I shouldn't go back into teaching. I wasn't following any kind of path that would get me to that goal, even though I knew deep down that reaching it would make me successful, at least how I defined it. In my heart, I knew I wasn't reaching my full potential as a human being. My paycheck might have said otherwise, but my definition of success has never been tied to money. For me, success means making a real difference in someone's life. That's why I chose a teaching career in the first place, and it's why I spent my first six years out of college trying to help students succeed.

Unfortunately, back then I was young and stupid. I couldn't handle the psychological complexities of the teaching profession. When you're a teacher, you're also a father (or mother), a mentor, a psychologist, a disciplinarian and, most importantly, a salesman. When I was fresh out of school, the kids I was teaching weren't that much younger than I was, and I just didn't have the life experience to teach them anything more meaningful than the lesson plan in front of me.

Money was much more important to me then than it is today, and I'll admit that the size of my bank account back in my twenties was a source of constant frustration. I wanted more money, but the real reason I left teaching was that I just didn't know enough to really inspire the kids.

Teaching Outside the Box

Today, I'm a much better teacher than I was before. It's truly my passion, and I take great joy in pushing kids to realize all that they're capable of. The experiences I've had in the "real world" give me a good understanding of what it takes to be successful. Colleges and universities do an outstanding job at providing intellectual stimulation, but they do a horrible job of giving young adults the skills they need to survive.

One major advantage of teaching in a smaller school is that the administrators are much more open to letting us think outside the box. Many larger schools make their faculty members teach the same subjects in exactly the same way. In my opinion, this stifles the learning process and makes kids lose interest, not only in school but also in everything else that's important. This type of one-size-fits-all teaching style may make sense on paper in a government bureaucracy, but I think it's pretty dangerous in actual practice. It can take the passion out of kids' lives, which I believe is a key ingredient to success. So even if most of the people at my high school thought I was crazy for coming up with my McDonald's Diet, to their credit they were willing to let me give it a shot. This McDonald's thing would never fly in a bigger district.

The Colo-NESCO school district is actually quite advanced when it comes to implementing new strategies to improve learning outcomes for students. Just a couple of years ago, we received a grant to explore the educational benefits of one-to-one learning, using tablets, the cloud and mobile apps. Today, every junior high school student in Colo gets an iPad, and the high school students get MacBook Pros. This kind of cutting-edge technology is helping us encourage life-long learning skills in our students, by giving them access to incredibly powerful tools they can take with them virtually anywhere. When I left teaching 25 years ago, technology in the classroom meant having an overhead projector. I bet most of my current students don't even know what that is!

Colo is a great place for me to teach because I'm passionate about what I do. Unfortunately, however, even such a great quality as passion has its downside. Sometimes when I feel particularly strong about something, the filter between my brain and my lips simply disintegrates. Actually, this happens quite often!

It seems that every few weeks I find myself getting called to the principal's office to face an angry parent who's upset about something I said or did that they found inappropriate. Usually, they're right! In these meetings I normally agree that my actions and/or words were uncalled for in the classroom, and I assure all interested parties that it will never happen again.

While I learn my lesson each time and never make the same mistake twice, I inevitably find some other way to end up back in Principal Kelley's office. It would save me a lot of legwork if I just set up my office next to his! I make light of this, not because I think I'm right, but because the reasons for my indiscretions have everything to do with my mission to help all of my students become successful.

It really frustrates me when students don't care — especially the ones who have the talent to do something truly great with their lives. I've been in the real world long enough to know that there are thousands of people out there with potential who never turn it into anything else. I don't want that for my students. If they could only see what I've seen throughout my life, I know their attitudes would change. That's the challenge in teaching: you have to find the individual button within every kid that will motivate them to do better than they ever thought possible.

Principal Kelley and I have gone round and round over this subject on more than one occasion. He takes the stance that schools exist for one purpose — to educate the kids. I agree with that statement, but I guess my definition of education is different from that of most administrators. School districts put so much importance on academic testing and "learning the facts" that they've almost forgotten about teaching life skills.

In the world after school, there are very few second chances when you choose not to do something asked of you. There are lots of second chances for people who fail, however. Failure shows that you tried, and I deeply believe that the type of failure that occurs when you do your best is the active ingredient that can ultimately lead to success.

I know that I can't force a kid to want to be educated. But I can create so many ways for my students to learn that the only way they won't learn is if they choose not to do so. I'm a huge fan of a wonderful app called Educreations Interactive Whiteboard. While I'm teaching, it records my voice and captures everything I write on my iPad, which the students are also viewing in the front of the classroom. After each class, I put the lecture on my website for my students to review at their convenience.

Before every one of my tests I review every single thing my students will have to know. If a student simply pays attention in class and then looks at the review sessions online, by osmosis alone they should do well on my tests. I spend lots of time preparing these reviews to give students an avenue they can follow — if they choose — to be successful.

On one of the first tests I gave during my first year at Colo, one of my classes did very poorly. "How many of you listened to the review before the test?" I asked my students the following day. Out of a class of 25, three hands went up.

"Gang, that really pisses me off," I complained, feeling my blood pressure rising. I stepped up on my soapbox and gave them the accountability speech, the choice speech and the it's-impossible-to-fail-my-class-if-you'd-only-take-advantage-of-the-tools-I-give-you-to-be-successful speech. I was on fire. My students looked up at me wide-eyed, with mouths hanging open.

I didn't realize how much the word "pisses" would piss people off in Colo, Iowa. I got a scathing e-mail from one parent, who copied Principal Kelley. It was off to his office the next morning, and I told the parent that she was absolutely, 100-percent correct that I shouldn't have used that type of language in class. I went on to explain why I said what I did, and how sometimes my intense desire for getting kids to achieve made me do things without thinking first. Despite the fanny chewing I got from that mom that morning, I give her credit for having the guts to address me directly. She and I have a great relationship, and the confrontation we had has made me a better teacher.

I certainly don't have all the answers in life, but I do know that hard work, discipline and a passion for excellence in whatever you do can set you up for success and help you live a life with few, if any, regrets. Those qualities don't guarantee that you'll achieve your goals, or that you won't suffer from an unfortunate twist of fate, but they can put you in the strongest possible position to grab the brass ring and overcome many problems.

It was in that mindset that I opened the door of the McDonald's in Nevada, Iowa, on the morning of September 16, 2013, and ordered the first meal of my McDonald's Diet.

Chapter 4: Choosing the Food, Glorious Food

"I once ate McDonald's three times in one day."
— Christina Ricci

"Hi John," the woman said as I walked into the Nevada McDonald's on the first day of the experiment.

"Good morning!" I replied, cheerfully.

"Are you ready to get started?"

"You bet! I'll have a Sausage Burrito, a Fruit & Maple Oatmeal and a small orange juice," I said. I told her that I also needed to get a Premium Southwest Salad, a Fruit 'N Yogurt Parfait and two orders of Apple Slices. That was going to be my lunch later in the day.

"And you got my promo code?" I asked.

"You're all set, John. Good luck!" She handed me two bags filled with food.

I thanked her and walked back to my car to resume my commute to Colo. I turned on the ignition and looked at my first McDonald's meal. It seemed like a fine choice to me. I could smell the warm aroma of the steaming burrito as it wafted up to my nostrils when I opened the bag. The eggs and the sausage offered a fair amount of protein, and it tasted great.

The oatmeal was equally delicious and it gave me a good source of dietary fiber. There was another bonus: oatmeal is what they call a low glycemic index (GI) carbohydrate, which means it releases glucose into the bloodstream more slowly than the kind of carbohydrates found in other cereals, like corn flakes and puffed rice. Many people believe that eating more low GI carbohydrates can help stabilize your blood sugar and reduce your risk of getting type 2 diabetes. I was off to a great start!

I got to know the employees of the McDonald's in Nevada, Iowa — like Katie — pretty well during my 90-day experiment. Now when they see me coming, they have my meals ready before I get to the counter!

Balanced Days vs. Balanced Meals

Since the mid-2000s, McDonald's and other fast food restaurants have added quite a bit of variety to their menus, including healthier choices like oatmeal, salads, fruit snacks and grilled sandwiches. By the second week of my diet, for example, I had discovered the Egg White Delight McMuffin. It's a healthier spin on the famous Egg McMuffin, with only 250 calories and 18 grams of protein. Compared to its older brother, the Egg White Delight has nearly half the fat and 40 fewer calories.

That particular breakfast entrée became a staple of my McDonald's Diet. Eating it in the morning along with a bowl of oatmeal, and choosing things like Fruit 'N Yogurt Parfaits, salads and apple slices for lunch, allowed me to "indulge" in the more traditional burger sandwiches, fries and even sundaes at dinner. Now, I'm not a nutritionist and I'm well aware of the conventional wisdom that says you shouldn't eat your heavier meals at night, but this is what worked for me. I was more interested in my total daily calories than I was about when I ate them.

It was really a function of how my days were structured and where I got my food that led to my pattern of treating myself to the occasional Deluxe Quarter Pounder, Big Mac and Hot Fudge Sundae during my evening meals. In the mornings, I'd stop into the McDonald's in Nevada, Iowa on my drive to work and take my breakfast and lunch to go. I'd usually eat my breakfast during my commute, and throw my lunch in the lab refrigerator when I got to school. Because I ordered my lunch at 7:15 in the morning, I couldn't have had a burger if I wanted to because the restaurant wasn't making them at that early hour.

Remember, this is Iowa, not New York where there's a McDonald's every three or four blocks. The McDonald's I go to is six miles from my high school, and I didn't have time to make that drive back and forth in the middle of the day. So instead, I contented myself with the menu items that were available and that could stay fresh in the fridge for several hours.

By dinnertime I was usually pretty hungry. After lunch I had to finish the school day, help coach the football team and do my daily 45 minutes of exercise. It was usually after 6:00 p.m. when I began my drive back to McDonald's. When I got to the restaurant about a half hour later, I took the opportunity to sit down with a hot meal and decompress with the newspaper before driving the remaining 40 miles back home. I also thought that my lingering at McDonald's would give my wife and daughters the chance to eat whatever they were going to have for dinner without tempting me or feeling guilty about eating in front of me.

Well, was I wrong about that! My beautiful wife and daughters were merciless, waving my favorite foods in front of my face every chance they got and asking me if I wanted any. One time, they ordered a pizza and all I got to do was lick the outside of the box! All my life I've been a joker, and I was learning that paybacks really are hell. But I deserved it, and even enjoyed it. Their behavior made me laugh, and in a strange way I was proud that they had adopted my sense of humor. Charlie Chaplin once said that "a day without laughter is a day wasted," and I couldn't agree more.

The Spice of Life

One of the reasons I chose McDonald's for this experiment over other fast food establishments was the fact that they do offer such a wide variety of menu items. I did my due diligence and looked at menus from Wendy's, Burger King, KFC and others, but for various reasons they weren't optimal for me. KFC has no breakfast items and no salads. Burger King and Wendy's have no items with egg whites. Little things like that made me stick to my instincts, and stick with the Golden Arches. I'm sure you could do a version of my diet at any fast food restaurant, but I liked the selection McDonald's offered and I thought I'd have the best chance at getting halfway decent nutrition.

It was pretty easy for me to check out the menus and nutrition information for all the other restaurant chains in the area. Laws regulating the disclosure of nutrition facts now require fast food chains across the country to communicate calorie counts and other nutrient values. Pretty much every restaurant has this information in-store and online. While perhaps a minor inconvenience for the restaurant chains, disclosing this information really has had an impact on the health of the nation. Numerous studies have shown that when people look at the nutrition facts labeling, they actually do order food with fewer calories.

My students and I relied heavily on the McDonald's website, which has a great user interface for calculating nutrition information. You can go to mcdonalds.com right now and use the Meal Builder to add up the calories and other nutritional values for any combination of items you want. It's actually kind of fun, and if you have young kids it's a great way to teach them about making sensible food choices.

While I never once got tired of the food at McDonald's, I have to admit that Chicken McNuggets and Filet-o-Fish sandwiches aren't among my favorites. On the other hand, I pretty much enjoyed eating everything else, especially the Egg White Delights and the new Bacon Habanero Ranch Quarter Pounder. My students did a fantastic job of mixing things up for me throughout the experiment and making sure that many of my favorite foods were on the daily menus. To see everything that I ate during my McDonald's Diet, go to the daily menu section at the back of the book.

A Fortunate Encounter

I feel incredibly lucky to have met Kevin O'Brien, the McDonald's franchisee who's dating my wife's best friend. We hit it off right away and developed an easy rapport. We both enjoy baseball. We both have a marketing background. And neither of us are big fans of the documentary *Super Size Me*.

But for Kevin, it's kind of personal. His family has been in the burger business since 1958, when his mother became the first female franchisee in the McDonald's system. When *Super Size Me* came out in 2004, the movie got a lot of play in the local schools. Kevin first found out about the movie after his son saw the film in class! Kevin reached out to the administrators at his son's school and asked if he could come in to present his side of the story. He wanted to help kids realize that anything in excess isn't going to be good for you. The school let him come in, and he was happy that most of the kids he talked to were skeptical as to why Morgan Spurlock would want to deliberately hurt himself just to tarnish the reputation of a company.

I was bursting with enthusiasm when I first mentioned my experiment to Kevin, because I knew he'd be into it as much as I was.

"Slow down!" he said. "Just take a breath and take me through the whole thing."

I explained everything about the experiment, and when he realized it was the exact opposite of *Super Size Me*, he was on board. I made it clear to him that, while I expected positive results, I was going to be totally honest about what happened to me over the course of the three months. That included making my blood work public, and no one — not even me — had any idea how that would turn out.

Kevin understood the parameters of my experiment and was confident enough in his products to give me his full support. The only problem was that his franchise locations were not the most convenient for me. I wanted to use the McDonald's in the town of Nevada because it was on my way to work. Kevin said that he'd put in a good word for me with the owner, a guy named Jim Baker, who was also a close friend of Kevin's.

Jim was open to the idea, but I think he was concerned that I might be trying to set them up in some way. Kevin assured him that I wasn't out to get them. I didn't have an agenda, and I wasn't going to turn myself into a glutton like Morgan Spurlock did. Kevin vouched for me as a stand-up guy and explained that I was a former corporate executive who was now teaching science at the high school in Colo. He told Jim that this was for a semester project in my sophomore biology class. He explained that I was limiting my calories to 2,000 a day, that we were targeting a whole set of nutritional values to be as close to the RDA as possible and that I'd be exercising 45 minutes a day as part of the experiment. Kevin knew that McDonald's had good food on its menu, and he thought they couldn't lose.

While Kevin worked to convince Jim to go along with the idea, I was getting just a little bit nervous. The experiment's start date was fast approaching and I hadn't heard a thing. I called Kevin to find out what was going on, and he told me to sit tight.

It was September 12 when Jim Baker called me up to introduce himself. He apologized for not getting back to me sooner.

"No problem," I lied.

He asked me if we could meet to discuss my idea in person.

"Of course!" I went over to his McDonald's right away to tell him everything.

Jim introduced me to Joe Roney, the supervisor at the Nevada location, and also to Heidi Fisher, one of the managers.

I could barely squeeze myself into the table where they were all sitting because I was so big, but once I got myself situated I explained what my experiment was all about. They listened politely, and I would have loved to know what was going on inside their heads. Did they look at me and think that I'd never have the self-control to see this thing through? Or did they say to themselves that this guy couldn't possibly gain any more weight, so why not help him out?

When I first started my McDonald's Diet I could barely squeeze myself into the seats.

"Okay," Jim finally said. "We'll do it."

They gave me a promo code to use for my food. I thanked them profusely and told them that they'd be seeing a lot less of me over the next three months. We all laughed and shook hands, and I went back home to pig out for a few more days on my usual diet of 4,000-plus calories.

Before I dove into my first bag of kettle chips, I told Kevin how much I appreciated his help setting everything up for me. He wished me well, and asked me to keep him in the loop regarding my weight and my blood work.

"You got it, buddy," I said. "Wish me luck!"

"You're going to do just fine," he said. "I have faith in our food!"

Here I am with my patrons of the culinary arts, Kevin O'Brien (right) and Jim Baker.

The Good Ol' Boy Gang

One of the things that surprised me about eating at McDonald's for 90 days was how solitary the experience was. Meals are ordinarily such social occasions, but I was pretty much on my own in this experiment. Sure, I had lunch with my colleagues at school every day and they gave me a good ribbing each time they saw me coming with my McDonald's sack in hand, but breakfast and dinner were typically private affairs. I always had my morning meal in the car, and I never invited anyone — nor did anyone ask — to have dinner with me at McDonald's during the course of the experiment. I didn't mind the solitude, and perhaps I welcomed it because of how unusual my situation was and how hard I had to focus on sticking to the plan.

That's not to say that my experience was devoid of meaningful human contact. Obviously, I got to know the McDonald's employees very well. They've been with me on this journey more than anyone. And, because it was easier for them to ring me up at the front registers than at the Drive-Thru window for some reason due to my promo-code arrangement, I also got to know a group of people who seemed to go this same restaurant as much as I did.

About a dozen retirees from the community have been gathering at this particular McDonald's every day for the past 10 years. When they saw me coming in every day like clockwork, they began to get curious. One day, a few weeks into the diet, a couple of them came up to me and asked what I was up to. They must have found out from the employees that I was getting my food for free!

"That's interesting," said one of the guys when I explained the experiment. The other gave me an obligatory nod, but I could tell he thought I was nuts. Once again, I would have loved to know what they were thinking — and what they said about me to their group when I left!

It was actually quite comforting to see these guys having their coffee and sandwiches, and enjoying each other's company every morning. I looked forward to seeing them. You could tell that this group went way back with each other and that the bonds of friendship were strong. It made me feel good just to be around them and to feel the positive energy emanating out of the group.

Every day, when I walked into McDonald's and saw them, I'd say, "Good morning boys!"

They'd respond with a wave or a "How's it going today, John?" and we'd pretty much leave it at that.

It wasn't until the day after all the media went crazy that I realized how much of a part in this experiment they really played. They greeted me with an enthusiastic "Mr. Celebrity!" when I walked in the door of the McDonald's the first day after I got back from New York. They shared in my moment of glory and were sincerely happy for me. They asked me for my autograph and I told them I was only signing fat stomachs that day. About half of them qualified, but fortunately I didn't have any takers.

Sitting down for breakfast with the good ol' boy gang.

A Turkey of a Day

Throughout the experiment, every day was pretty much like any other. There was a comforting monotony during the three months that kept me going without a lot of distractions. I could handle the teasing from my colleagues, my students and my family. I could watch them eat their food without self-pity. I knew what I had to do each day and I followed through.

As my students and I were putting together the schedule for the experiment, however, I had a disturbing feeling about one particular day. I was like a professional athlete scanning the calendar for the most challenging opponents. In my case, I would face my fiercest enemy on day 74. It was Thursday, November 28 — otherwise known as Thanksgiving Day.

"It's just one day," I thought to myself. "How tough can it really be? I mean, every American League team has to play the Yankees at least once a year, and they seem to get through it okay. So why can't I get through Thanksgiving?"

This food-oriented holiday, which my wife and I have hosted for the past 10 years, is a big thing in the Cisna household. All the grandparents, aunts and uncles, nephews and nieces, and associated boyfriends and girlfriends flock to our humble abode for a magnificent feast.

Grandma Alice is the CEO of this event, and I swear she starts to plan each dinner about a year in advance. If you think Henry Ford's assembly line was efficient, you've never met Grandma Alice. She gives every person the responsibility for a specific item, and the resulting product is nothing short of extraordinary. Aunt Doris is in charge of bringing mass quantities of fresh-cut veggies with Italian dressing. We count on Grandma Sharon for the escalloped corn casserole. Uncle Dave and Aunt Dawn bring abundant cheese and cracker platters. And Grandma Alice takes care of the turkey, dressing, mashed potatoes, gravy and pumpkin pies by herself.

Every year, I willingly take on my responsibility of carving the turkey when it's fresh out of the oven. I'm usually quite full after this job, because I simply can't resist tasting more than a few mouthwatering pieces of the warm, juicy meat before it all gets arranged on the serving tray. I also deliberately leave a lot of turkey on the bone after the carving is complete, just so I can devour it all myself before dinner starts. By the time I sit down and help myself to the banquet with everyone else, it's safe to say that I've probably exceeded the 2,000 calories I now limit myself to every day.

The Thanksgiving meal itself has to add another few thousand calories to my already-stretched stomach, and then I usually cap it all off with huge slices of pumpkin pie topped with fluffy mounds of homemade whipped cream. Talk about a cheat day!

In addition to carving the bird, as head of the household it's my responsibility to say grace before the main meal begins. This past Thanksgiving I asked God to give me the strength to avoid saying what I was really thinking about the McDonald's meal that sat on my plate while everyone around me was getting ready to dive into all their homemade goodies like animals. I got through the prayer just fine, although I may have lingered a bit longer than usual so they'd all have to wait.

At the beginning of the meal we pass everything clockwise, so I had to stare longingly at the merry-go-round of deliciousness that paraded by me. Laura, my youngest daughter, was seated to my right, and she giggled like a Munchkin from Oz every time she handed me a bowl, dish or platter.

I could've gone out of the house. I could've hidden in my room. I could've refused to host the meal this one time. But I didn't do any of those things. Instead, I enjoyed my small order of World Famous Fries, tried hard to appreciate my Filet-o-Fish sandwich (making a note to reprimand the kids for that one), and savored every bubbly sip of my large Diet Coke® while 13 of the people most dear to me in the world tore into their food like they hadn't eaten for days.

I ate as leisurely as I could, selecting my fries one by one and chewing my Filet-o-Fish so thoroughly that it liquefied before going down my throat. I even licked the tartar sauce that spilled off the sandwich from the side of the box it came in. Despite my best efforts, I still finished about two hours before everyone else!

Once this turkey of a day finally ended, I knew that the rest of the experiment was going to be a real success. I was in the home stretch! I only had 16 more days to go in the entire program. And people were starting to see that my crazy diet was getting results. Once folks realized that I stayed on my McDonald's Diet even during Thanksgiving, the experiment gained huge amounts of validity.

And you know, I really did have a wonderful time that day. It wasn't easy, but I did it. And it made me realize that the most important thing about Thanksgiving isn't the food, it's the people you surround yourself with.

Chapter 5: Sweating it Out

"Get comfortable with being uncomfortable."
—Jillian Michaels

Every nutritionist will tell you that a balanced diet and moderate physical activity are the keys to being healthy. So, in addition to my sensible 2,000 daily calories from McDonald's, my students and I decided that I should walk for 45 minutes a day, four or five days a week, as part of the experiment. We wanted to make our program accessible to everyone if it worked, and we felt that most people would be able to get their physical activity by walking, versus other activities like running or lifting weights. We wanted to keep this thing as simple as possible, so people wouldn't need a degree from MIT to understand it.

Being the former jock that I was, I thought that the exercise part of the experiment would be a lot easier than the diet. In fact, performing physical activity was the least of my worries when we were in the planning stages of the experiment. We decided on 45 minutes because a half-hour seemed too little for burning off enough fat, and an hour seemed like it could get in the way of my other responsibilities and cut into my sleep time. The only way I could reasonably fit exercise into my schedule was to use the school track from 5:15 p.m. – 6:00 p.m., after coaching the junior-high football team. It would mean getting home later than usual most days, but I figured it would be time well spent. Remember my before picture!

I've since learned that CDC guidelines for healthy adults age 18 to 64 call for at least 2-1/2 hours (150 minutes) of moderate-intensity aerobic activity, such as the kind of brisk walking I was doing, each week. Other acceptable activities include water aerobics, bike riding, doubles tennis and mowing the lawn. For even greater health benefits, the CDC recommends at least 5 hours (300 minutes) of moderate-intensity aerobic activity per week. I also learned that you can still get health benefits even if you have to break your exercise sessions down into segments as short as 10 minutes each.

I was happy with the way we structured my routine, and I ended up walking between 180 and 225 minutes a week. I was ahead of the basic CDC guidelines, but not quite up to the level of activity recommended for greater health benefits. Truth be told, I was pretty much right where I needed to be for my fitness level at the time. I think if I had known about these guidelines before I got started, my ego would have pushed me to try for higher amounts of activity, and I would have really been in sorry shape.

One thing I didn't incorporate into my routine was strength training. Again, the goal was to make the plan accessible to as large a population as possible. However, the CDC recommends full-body strength workouts on two or more days a week, in addition to their guidelines for aerobic exercise. Whether you lift weights, work with resistance bands, do calisthenics like push-ups and sit-ups, take a yoga class, or even do heavy gardening, you want to try and work all the major muscle groups: your legs, hips, back, abs, chest, shoulders and arms.

Since the first part of my experiment ended, I've incorporated strength training into my exercise regimen. It's made a big difference, and I feel almost as good today as I did when I was playing ball in college. In chapter 8, I'll tell you all about my new, higher-intensity routine.

A Good Walk Spoiled

The first day out on the track was a beautiful September evening. It was one of those perfect, late-summer twilights that just make you feel happy to be alive. I was all set and ready to go. I had my video camera rolling, and my trusty stopwatch was by my side. Everything was in place for a remarkable evening that I would remember fondly forever.

After about 25 minutes into my walk, I started looking behind me to see who kept hitting the back of my legs with a 2 x 4. I wasn't feeling good at all, and it crossed my mind that I may not actually be able to walk the full 45 minutes. I nervously looked around to make sure there were other people around in case I needed medical attention. I tried to tough it out, and even ran through some of the commands I bark at my junior-high football players when they're struggling to keep up in practice. Not five minutes later I came to a complete stop.

My mind may have been saying yes, but my body was saying "Holy Buckets, Batman!" Carrying 280 pounds around for any length of time was a lot harder than I thought it would be. There were turtles that could lap me around the track!

On my first day out on the track I could only walk for 30 minutes.

What in the world had I gotten myself into? I was beginning to worry that I should have at least seen a doctor before starting this whole thing, to see if I was in any kind of shape to try to get in shape. I saw my doctor for my blood work, but that was it. What was I thinking?!

If you're planning to start a regular exercise program, The American College of Sports Medicine says that you should see a doctor if you can say yes to two or more of the following conditions:

- You're a man older than age 45 or a woman older than age 55
- You have a family history of heart disease before age 55

- You smoke or you quit smoking in the past six months
- You haven't exercised for three months or more
- You're overweight or obese
- You have high blood pressure or high cholesterol
- You have impaired glucose tolerance, also called prediabetes

I could have checked off my age, lack of exercise and obesity right off the bat, and my first blood work revealed that I also had high cholesterol.

It may seem silly to go to your doctor before you start exercising if you generally feel healthy, but exercising after a long break — or for the first time ever — can be a shock to your system. If you haven't exercised in a while, physical activity can cause elevated blood pressure and other cardiovascular problems, not to mention musculoskeletal injuries if you dive into your new program with too much enthusiasm.

The specific tests you should get depend on your current condition and your specific fitness goals. Consider getting a comprehensive evaluation that includes a review of past medical problems, a look at your family medical history, comprehensive blood tests and possibly an exercise stress test.

While I was disappointed in myself for only making two-thirds of my 45-minute goal that first night, what really bummed me out was the thought of what it was going to feel like the next morning just to get out of bed. Sure enough, as soon as my feet hit the floor the next day I felt like a newborn colt trying to find the strength just to stand. The last thing I wanted to do was have to pick up my 280 pounds off the bedroom floor, and my wife got a kick out watching me find my footing.

If I had died that morning, I think I would have felt better. It was such an ordeal getting out of bed, and there I was with 89 more days to go. I really didn't know if I could make it.

But, as you know, I persevered. By the end of the first week I was walking two and a quarter miles and could go without stopping for 40 minutes. If I do the math right that's 3.375 miles an hour, which was a whole lot better than when I started. During the next week I was able to walk for the full 45 minutes, and after that I kept covering more ground in the same timeframe.

Roaming the Halls

Up until the midway point of the experiment the weather cooperated and I did all my workouts outside on the track. But by the end of October, things had changed. It was in the 80s one day, and in the 40s the next, with the wind blowing out of the northwest at about 35 miles an hour. At that point it was no longer exercise. It was survival. I felt like Les Stroud from *Survivorman*. I was filming all my exercise sessions myself, after all!

When it got too cold and windy, I decided to move my workouts inside the school.

Knowing that the weather was only going to get worse as fall progressed, I moved my little dog and pony show inside after the fifth week. If I thought walking around the track was boring, walking the empty hallways of the school was absolutely miserable. It was incredibly lonely and monotonous. Don't get me wrong, the janitors were very friendly, but it's not like we could all stop what we were doing for a little chat.

So I just slogged away, my footsteps echoing around me in the abandoned halls. I was bored out of my mind. I know some people listen to music or books on tape when they exercise, but I'm just not that type of person.

Fortunately, the exercise actually started to become fun once I started losing a significant amount of weight. By day 60, exactly two-thirds of the way through the experiment, I weighed 28 pounds lighter than when I started. I was able to walk the 45 minutes at a much brisker pace, and the increased intensity encouraged even more weight loss. I was sweating, not because I couldn't handle the activity, but because I was starting to push myself a little harder by moving faster, changing my route throughout the hallways, and even climbing up and down the occasional stairway.

Once I lost 28 pounds halfway through the diet, the exercise started getting fun.

Chapter 6: The Results — Who's Laughing Now?

"He started to sing as he tackled the thing
That couldn't be done, and he did it."
— Edgar Albert Guest, *It Couldn't Be Done*

At the end of the experiment I weighed 243.2 pounds, for a total of 37 pounds lost. My chest measured 44 inches, down from 48.5. My hips went down from 49 inches to 45, and my stomach shrank seven inches, stretching the tape to just 44 inches instead of 51.

I was still a big guy, but the transformation was enough to cause a lot of commotion around campus and throughout the community — especially when my story hit the local news on KCCI. I can't go anywhere today without someone recognizing me as the guy who eats McDonald's. I think it's my haircut that gives me away!

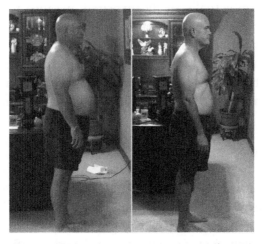

What a difference eating at McDonald's makes!

Kevin O'Brien and Jim Baker, the franchisees who helped make this experiment possible, were probably the most flabbergasted of all — not because they didn't believe in their food, but because they didn't see me at all during the experiment. They didn't want to have any impact on what I was doing, and I didn't want anyone to think we weren't being completely honest and objective. Although I kept them apprised of my situation via email, I think they simply got caught up in other things and weren't even giving me a second thought as the weeks went by. As long as I wasn't getting sick or dying, they had no reason to worry about my experiment. So when the three months were over and they physically saw with their own eyes how much weight I had lost, they simply couldn't believe it.

But even my students, who had the benefit of seeing me day in and day out carrying my McDonald's bags all the time and doing my lonely walk on the track or through the halls, were also pretty astonished when it was all over.

Sophomore Morgan Dunahoo, for example, who only thought of "grease and the salty French fries" when someone mentioned McDonald's, was aware of my experiment and watched my slow and sometimes painful transformation. "I could see Mr. Cisna walking," she said. "At the beginning he struggled, but at the end it was easy for him."

Michael Starling, the student who called me an idiot at the start of the experiment, was perhaps the most impressed with my transformation. "Now that I've seen the results I'm actually really surprised, because I didn't think Mr. Cisna could lose that much weight," he said to my video camera. "Losing it all at McDonald's is kind of a big deal because everybody I know who goes there just thinks it's terrible, and for him to be able to do that is just crazy. For Mr. Cisna to actually watch what he eats, and the calories, goes to show that it's not McDonald's that's making us fat and our bodies unhealthy, its just how much we consume and what we consume."

Give that kid an A+!

Another student, Ricki Grover, also understood what I was trying to achieve through my experiment. "You can eat wherever you want as long as you're making the right decisions," she realized. "If you're going to eat a Big Mac every single day you may gain some weight, but if you have more healthy stuff, or if you mix it up and make sure you're not eating 5,000 calories a day or something, then you can stay healthy eating at McDonald's."

Gosh, these kids in Colo are smart!

It all comes down to moderation, a concept my colleague Dana Accola constantly tries to get through to the students who take his family consumer science class. "It's not that you can't have a cookie or a piece of pie, it's just that you don't want to eat the whole plate of cookies or the whole pie itself," he says. "It's our decision not to purchase that salad that hurts us more than anything."

People were definitely singing a different tune about my experiment when the story hit the news. I admire the people around me for their candor and honesty, and for their willingness to admit that they were wrong about what I was doing. It was gratifying to see how people, especially the students, were able to acknowledge that their preconceived notions got in the way of the truth.

I knew before the experiment started that it was mathematically impossible for me not to lose weight on a 2,000-calorie-a-day diet, whether I ate at McDonald's or at Whole Foods.

But again, the big unknown — the heart of our hypothesis — was whether or not I could lose the weight in a healthy manner by eating nothing but McDonald's for breakfast, lunch and dinner for 90 days. One might argue that thinner automatically means healthier, but we wouldn't know for sure until we got my blood work back.

Becoming More "Desirable"

At the start of the experiment, my total cholesterol was 249 mg/dL. My LDL was 170 mg/dL, my triglycerides were 156 mg/dL and my cholesterol-to-HDL ratio was 5.19:1.

These numbers were not good. They told me that I was at a much greater risk for heart disease than I wanted to be. According to the Mayo Clinic, cholesterol levels above 240 mg/dL are considered high, and you have to get them all the way down to 200 mg/dL to be in the "desirable" range. My LDL of 170 mg/dL was also in the "high" range. The only good news in my lab report was my triglycerides number, which was only "borderline high."

Grant Tiarks, one of the students conducting the experiment with me, suggested we get my blood work at the halfway point of the experiment in addition to the beginning and the end. We all thought that was a good idea, because it would give us a good indication if things were going in the right direction.

So on November 1st, I had my blood drawn and waited for the results to come in the mail. When the lab report arrived, we were so shocked that I actually called the doctor's office to make sure what they sent me was indeed correct.

My doctor confirmed the accuracy of the numbers: my cholesterol was down to 189 mg/dL and in the "desirable" range. Similarly, my LDL was down to 129 mg/dL — "near ideal" — and my triglycerides were down to a "desirable" 94 mg/dL. My glucose level was a little higher than it was when I started, but it was still in the "desirable" range at 87 mg/dL.

We began to realize that we were onto something big. I shared those halfway results with some of my colleagues and they were as shocked as I was. Having these amazing numbers really gave me a much-needed mental boost to finish the experiment to its exact specifications. And, combined with the superficial changes that were starting to become noticeable, the positive lab report got people to start playing a more active role in watching what we were doing.

During the last week of the experiment, I went in for my final blood test. I wanted to have the results in hand on the last day, when I would step on the scale for the final time. When I got the lab report I almost started to cry. At that moment, it finally hit me that my commitment and all the hard work I needed to do to fulfill it had paid off, in spite of the fact that so many people thought it would be a total waste of time.

The final blood work came back phenomenal. My total cholesterol was down 32 percent from the beginning of the experiment. My triglycerides dropped by 49 percent. My LDL was down 34 percent and my cholesterol-to-HDL ratio dropped 20 percent. I was indeed getting healthier on my McDonald's Diet!

Fig. 2

My McDonald's Diet Blood Work

	9/16/13	11/1/13	12/14/13
Total Cholesterol	249 mg/dL	189 mg/dL	170 mg/dL
LDL	170 mg/dL	129 mg/dL	113 mg/dL
Triglycerides	156 mg/dL	94 mg/dL	80 mg/dL
Chol/HDL	5.19:1	4.61:1	4.15:1

Friends in Hy-Vee Places

When I received my lab report at the midpoint of the experiment, I contacted two health and diet professionals from the dietitian nutrition services division of Hy-Vee, one of the largest grocery store chains in Iowa. Katie Jackson and Anne Hytrek are both full-time, registered dietitians. Katie is also certified in Adult Weight Management and Anne is a Certified Diabetes Educator with a Masters in Science Education.

Both of these women and their colleagues provide a far-reaching array of nutrition counseling and education programs for individuals, families, students and even businesses. Their goal is to help people understand nutrition labels, make better food choices and find out if they're at risk for heart disease, diabetes and other chronic conditions.

Registered dietitians Katie Jackson (left) and Anne Hytrek believe my McDonald's Diet can help people who've been frustrated by diets in the past.

When I told them what I was doing and showed them all the data we collected from the menus, lab reports and workout logs, they were really intrigued.

They understood that the experiment we conducted could help a lot of regular people who may be frustrated by different diets or who beat themselves up for breaking down and having a burger when they should be sticking to their weight-loss program. What my McDonald's Diet proves is that as long as the big picture is in balance, it's okay if some meals fall short in the number of vitamins or have too much fat.

"Before John's experience, I tended to tell clients to minimize their dining out to 1 or 2 days per week if possible, sometimes less," Katie commented. "However, after seeing John's success story, I've come to appreciate what McDonalds, and other restaurants, have to offer to the public."

"We can't expect people to eat perfectly balanced meals all the time," added Anne. "But we might be able to get them to balance out their days, like John did. His daily menus can be really helpful in showing people that even unhealthy choices can fit into their overall day, as long as they're making healthy choices, as well."

Katie and Anne both believe that my program can be especially useful for people who feel so guilty when they break their diet that they give up entirely and start binging on unhealthy foods. "What you did can really help people understand that one or two unhealthy meals won't hurt their overall health or weight," Katie told me. "Our goal as registered dietitians is to help customers break the cycle of stress that leads to poor eating habits, and we can do this by helping them realize that one 'bad' meal or snack will not hurt their diet."

"Normally, we like to educate consumers on eating the MyPlate way," said Anne. This is a portion control system that lets you fill half your plate with fruits and vegetables, one-quarter of your plate with lean protein and the other quarter of your plate with whole grain and healthy fats or oils.

"You didn't follow this formula," Katie reminded me, "but your diet did meet your RDA needs overall and we were pleasantly surprised to see that the variety of food you consumed led to positive health changes … I think the main message from the experiment is that … we all have a choice, and that when we go out to eat at these fast food restaurants it's about what we choose on the menu. If someone wants to come in for some fries, maybe they pair them with a salad or apple slices instead of a Big Mac."

Anne concurred, saying that "most people have a pre-set idea of what they usually order at these types of places … I think this type of experiment shows that when you choose different, healthier food options, you can make all foods fit."

I couldn't have agreed more, and at the end of the experiment I was ready to share it with the world.

Chapter 7: No Big Macs
   in the Big Apple

*"One belongs to New York instantly, one belongs to it as
much in five minutes as in five years."*
— Tom Wolfe

Looking back, I don't know if I would have been as successful during my 48 hours in New York City if I had had any time to prepare for the trip. Everything happened to me so quickly that I really wasn't able to dwell on the anxieties I was feeling during my stay in the Big Apple. If I had had even a minute to slow down and take it all in as the events were unfolding, I probably would have had a nervous breakdown. Instead, I had to think on my feet, look for help where I could find it, go with the flow and ultimately shut off my cell phone.

My plane flew into LaGuardia Airport at about 9:30 p.m. I love flying into cities at night. The lights from the buildings and the roads are so dramatic, shining from the darkness like a million twinkling, shooting stars. LaGuardia was buzzing with activity even at that late hour, as I walked from the gate to whatever experiences awaited me. The first of those experiences manifested itself in the form of a guy who reminded me of Kato from *The Green Hornet*. My limo driver was holding a sign with my name on it, and he drove me, in total silence — and luckily with no need for hand-to-hand combat or green sleeve darts — to the Club Quarters Hotel on West 51st St.

Like most hotels in Manhattan, the rooms at the Club Quarters were models of efficiency. Mine contained a bed and a table, and that was pretty much it. But when you're in New York City, who wants to stay in a hotel room? Me, that's who! It was closing in on 10:30 p.m., and my call time at the *TODAY* show was six o'clock in the morning. Fortunately, the hotel was conveniently located near most of the big studios, including NBC and Fox News, so if I got up at 5:00 a.m. I'd have enough time to shower, shave and walk over to NBC.

Green Room Hunger Pangs

It was raining when I left the hotel the next morning, but I didn't mind. The temperature was a pleasant 56 degrees, and there were lots of people out and about. I had slept pretty well the night before once the adrenaline rush of just being there ran its course, and it was good to get my blood circulating in advance of my first big interview.

When I arrived at NBC studios just a little before 6:00 a.m., I told the security guard that I was there for the *TODAY* show.

"And you are?" he asked.

"John Cisna," I said.

He looked down at his clipboard and used his finger to scroll through a long list of people. My name was right there on the clipboard, and it caused his finger to stop. "Ah. There you are," he said. I was feeling pretty special as he called up to the studio.

After a few moments, the young lady I had spoken with on the phone just the day before came out to greet me.

"Hi, Mr. Cisna," she enthused, holding out her hand. "I'm so glad you made it!"

She was very nice and made me feel right at home as we headed to the green room, which is sort of a holding tank where guests can relax before they go on set. It's actually a pretty neat place, because right outside the big glass window is where they do all the outdoor scenes with weatherman Al Roker.

The green room was filled with just about every kind of breakfast item you could think of, from fruit and pastries of all kinds to donuts and breakfast sandwiches. Unfortunately, there were no Egg White Delights, no Fruit & Maple Oatmeals or anything else from McDonald's, so I had to do the show on an empty stomach.

I contented myself with a cup of black coffee and sat down. I felt relaxed and was confident that I'd do well on the show. As I was waiting, one of my favorite inspirational quotes came to mind. Mark Twain once said, "If you tell the truth, you don't have to remember anything." Everything about my McDonald's Diet experiment was backed by as much data as we could possibly have collected, so all I really had to do was let the numbers speak for themselves.

Talking Baseball with Bob Costas

After a few minutes, another lady came into the green room and told me to come with her.

"Where to?" I asked.

"Makeup," she said. I followed obediently and entered a brightly lit room with a line of chairs in front of four big mirrors — the kind with all the light bulbs around the perimeter. Each chair had a dedicated makeup artist, and I sat down where I was directed. I smiled at the woman who was going to make me look pretty, and offered a smart-aleck remark about not messing up my hair. She was not amused.

Without a word, she started putting stuff on my face. I made her job difficult by looking around a lot, just admiring the novelty of the situation. My makeup artist was somewhat annoyed with my behavior, but I'm glad I didn't sit still. As I turned to my right one time, I saw one of my all-time heroes: Bob Costas was being escorted into the chair next to mine!

As you know by now, I've been a huge baseball fan practically all of my life. One of my favorite films of all time is *Baseball*, the epic documentary by Ken Burns. If you ever want to know if you're talking to a true baseball fan, ask them if they've ever seen this movie. Only a true devotee of America's pastime would sit down and watch all 20+ hours of this masterpiece.

Bob Costas played a major role in this great documentary. His on-camera commentary on all aspects of the game demonstrates how much love and respect he has for the sport. Just read this quote of his from the movie, and you'll know how much of an impact baseball had on his life:

> *"Baseball is a human enterprise. Therefore, by definition, it's imperfect, it's flawed, it doesn't embody perfectly everything that's worthwhile about our country or about our culture. But it comes closer than most things in American life. And maybe this story,*

which is probably apocryphal, gets to the heart of it: An Englishman and an American are having an argument about something that has nothing to do with baseball. It gets to the point where it's irreconcilable, to the point of exasperation, and the American says to the Englishman, 'Ah, screw the king!' And the Englishman is taken aback, thinks for a minute and says, 'Well, screw Babe Ruth!' Now think about that. The American thinks he can insult the Englishman by casting aspersions upon a person who has his position by virtue of nothing except for birth; nothing to do with personal qualities, good, bad or otherwise. But who does the Englishman think embodies America? Some scruffy kid who came from the humblest of beginnings, hung out as a six-year-old behind his father's bar; a big, badly flawed, swashbuckling palooka, who strides with great spirit — not just talent, but with a spirit of possibility and enjoyment of life across the American stage. That's an American to the Englishman. You give me Babe Ruth over any king who's ever sat on the throne and I'll be happy with that trade."

Such eloquence! I could listen to Bob Costas talk about baseball all day long, and there he was not three feet away from me.

I seized the opportunity. "The greatest baseball documentary ever made is on my desktop back home," I said, turning in his direction while my makeup lady rolled her eyes.

He gave me a big smile. "Are you talking about the Ken Burns documentary?"

"Absolutely!" I exclaimed. "Mr. Costas, you were great in that film."

He shrugged it off. "Ken Burns made it easy."

We talked a little bit more about it, and he mentioned that his favorite person in the film was Buck O'Neil, Major League Baseball's first African-American coach.

"Yeah," I agreed. "He came across as somebody you just wanted to give a big hug to."

After his makeup was done, Mr. Costas got up and turned to me. "It was nice to meet you," he said. I could have died right then and there!

Swooning over Kathie Lee

Finally, it was my turn to leave the makeup chair and head to the studio. People were everywhere, scurrying around in crisscross directions like busy ants on important missions. Everyone in the studio was extremely focused on his or her individual responsibility. The whole operation ran like a well-oiled machine.

While I was waiting to go on the show, I noticed out of the corner of my eye that the beautiful Kathie Lee Gifford was standing just a few feet away from me. I turned to face her and stared for what seemed like an eternity. Then I managed to close my mouth, wipe the drool from my chin and muster up the courage to introduce myself. She graciously agreed to have her picture taken with me. "Wait till the people in Colo see this one," I thought to myself as I thanked Ms. Gifford and her colleagues profusely. I would have kept thanking them had I not been called to the set and whisked away by one of the assistant directors.

One of the highlights of my trip was meeting the beautiful Kathie Lee Gifford (right). With Willie Geist and Hoda Kotb.

All Hell Breaks Loose

My segment with Matt Lauer, Savannah Guthrie and Joy Bauer lasted exactly five minutes and one second. I felt good about how it all went, and everyone thanked me for doing a good job and being an interesting guest. Before I knew it, I was out the door and the program kept rolling forward. Like I said, the *TODAY* show was a well-oiled machine. Everyone I met at NBC was a consummate professional, and they all worked hard to make things run as smoothly and efficiently as humanly possible. After seeing these people in action I have a lot more respect for what it takes to run a top-tier network television operation, and I feel privileged to have been a part of it.

By the time I left NBC the rain had stopped and I was hoping to explore the big city. My next interview wasn't until the following morning on *Fox & Friends*, so I had the whole day ahead of me. Before doing anything else, however, I decided to go back to the hotel and wash all my makeup off. By the time I got to my room, half of it had already come off inside my hat!

I was on my way back to the Club Quarters Hotel when all hell broke loose. Emails started flooding into my phone, one right after another. The majority of the messages were requests for interviews from different newspapers, television shows and radio programs.

When I got back to the hotel, I tried to reply to each of these emails in the order that I received them but I just couldn't keep up. I was getting buried, and my anxiety level was starting to rise. My saving grace was an email I got from a company right in New York called United Stations Radio Networks. The woman who wrote the message offered to coordinate all my requests for radio interviews.

I quickly gave this nice lady a call and asked her what I needed to do to get this off my hands. She explained that they contracted with all the major radio shows across the country. She said that she'd contact these shows on my behalf, and also manage any specific requests that were coming my way.

"Okay," I said hesitantly. "How much is this going to cost me?"

There was a long pause on the other end of the line. "It won't cost you a thing," the woman finally said. I think she went into shock because I wasn't asking how much she'd be paying me for my leads! She must have known that I was totally overwhelmed and that I would have sucked pond water through a straw to get her to help me.

She asked me to send her what I had, and boy, was I relieved. With one thing off my plate I thought that things would die down a bit and I could finally take some time to walk around town. Wrong! The next email that caught my eye was from one of the producers of *Your World with Neil Cavuto* on Fox News. I gave her a call and she asked if I was still in New York.

"Yes," I said. "I'll be here until tomorrow night."

"Would you be interested in being a guest on Neil's show this afternoon?"

"Sure," I replied.

So much for tooling around Manhattan! Instead, I decided to get something to eat at McDonald's.

Before I could even leave the hotel room, however, my phone started ringing. It wasn't anyone I knew, which was a total surprise because I have an unlisted cell phone number. It was a producer from *Inside Edition*, who wanted to tape an interview with me the next afternoon.

"How did you get my phone number?" I asked.

"Uhh ..." she said, after a pause. "I got it off a website called extensionbaseballswing.com."

Then it hit me in the face like the heat from an oven when you open it up to take the cookies out. I forgot all about my little side venture, in which I give private hitting lessons to about 20 or 30 kids every year. (And no, I don't hit them with the ball like my dad did to me!) I created a website for this business so students and their parents can learn about what I have to offer and also see videos of what the kids' swings look like after they sign up for lessons. Lo and behold, right at the bottom of the home page is my personal email address and cell phone number.

Up until my *TODAY* show exposure, most of the news organizations had found me through my school e-mail address, which is easy to get if you Google

Colo-NESCO. But now I was hearing from people all around the world through my personal cell phone number and email address, too. My phone was going back and forth from one email account to another like dueling banjos. I realized that I had to stop extending my stay, because this media feeding frenzy was just not going to stop.

I shut off the phone and finally went to the McDonald's on 42nd Street, a short walk from my hotel. It occurred to me, as I was sitting down with my Grilled Chicken Premium McWrap, side salad and Diet Coke, that I was about to enjoy the first meal I'd eaten since I had breakfast at McDonald's in Iowa, more than 24 hours before. McDonald's food had never tasted so good!

An Enemy at the Gate?

With some satisfying fuel in the tank, I was feeling quite a bit calmer. I called the woman from United Stations and she told me that all my radio interviews were scheduled, starting at eight o'clock the next morning, after my *Fox & Friends* appearance. Everything was starting to fall into place again. I went back to the hotel and took a much-needed nap for about an hour and a half, and then got ready for my next interview with Neil Cavuto at Fox News studios.

Now, I'll be honest: I don't watch Fox News Channel that much. So when I entered their building on the Avenue of the Americas, I had visions of being forced to admit that I voted for Obama before being escorted out the back way, never to be heard from or seen again.

Well, not really, but based on my limited experience with the channel I wasn't sure what to expect. Let me tell you, Neil Cavuto turned out to be both a gentleman and a scholar. He was one of the nicest people who interviewed me, and he was the only one who sent me a handwritten thank-you note for appearing on his show. He's a classy guy through and through, and, as you know, he graciously agreed to write the foreword to this book.

I felt at ease with Neil right away, realizing that we had similar personalities and shared the same sense of humor. I could really be myself and joke around with him. When he pretended that he thought my diet consisted of 2,000 calories per meal — not per day — I was comfortable enough to say that 2,000 calories per meal is what got me looking like my before picture.

We had a good back and forth in the four minutes and 57 seconds we were together. "By the way, you could be eating at McDonald's for free for the rest of your life if you parlay this," he said to me at one point in the interview.

"Would you be my agent?" I replied.

"Absolutely. But I'd have to get a percentage," he said.

I hit it off with Fox News business anchor Neil Cavuto right away. He's one of the nicest guys you'll ever meet.

My freewheeling interview on *Your World with Neil Cavuto* was a nice way to end my first day in New York. My two appearances that day, first at NBC and then at Fox News, taught me that all great TV hosts are skilled at empathy. Matt Lauer, Savannah Guthrie and Neil Cavuto all have the ability to relate to any kind of guest who appears before them, and that's what makes for interesting interviews across the board.

My mind was racing from the day's experiences, but my body was begging for sleep. I was too tired to even think about getting dinner, which was funny, because earlier that day a producer from *Inside Edition* had asked me if I had any plans for eating out that night. Now normally, this would be a lead-in to some sort of an invitation, don't you think?

I told the producer that I had to find a McDonald's because I was still on the diet.

He looked at me kind of funny. "Really?" he wanted to know, before quickly excusing himself.

Needless to say, he never got back to me. It was just as well, because at that point I really didn't feel like eating or making small talk with anyone. I went back to my room and was out like a light by 7:30 p.m. in the city that never sleeps.

Learning from My Mistakes

The next morning I got up early again and headed back to Fox News. I had such a positive experience there the day before, and now it was familiar territory.

The hosts of *Fox & Friends* were all very pleasant and I felt comfortable about what I had to say. Once again, I thought about Mark Twain and his wise words about not having to remember anything if you tell the truth all the time. During this interview, however, I experienced a glitch that ticked me off a little bit. Co-host Steve Doocy took me off guard with a question about my midpoint results and I got a little flustered.

You see, I had provided all my data to the producers of all of the shows on which I appeared. They knew everything about my experiment, from my daily menus and exercise routine to my measurements and blood work. Most of the interviewers focused on my starting and ending numbers and I was used to talking about them. The *Fox & Friends* folks, however, took a slightly different approach and put up a graphic that showed my weight and cholesterol levels from the beginning, from the halfway point and from the end of the experiment. I wasn't as familiar with the midpoint numbers, so I stumbled a bit when Steve asked me to fill in the blanks like Richard Dawson used to do on *The Family Feud.*

Oh well, chalk it up to experience and to the pitfalls of live television. I regained my composure and the two-minute-thirty-two-second interview ended well, with co-host Brian Kilmeade joking that I'd be "wrestling at 126 this year."

On Fox & Friends, Steve Doocy (left) made me stumble a bit with a question about my midpoint numbers. With Elisabeth Hasselbeck and Brian Kilmeade.

A Radio Marathon

With my morning TV obligations over, I hopped a cab to the offices of United Stations to tell my story to various radio audiences. The lady I had been talking to welcomed me into the studio with a very familiar site — two Egg White Delights, a Fruit & Maple Oatmeal and a 1% milk. I really appreciated her willingness to go out of her way to get my breakfast. While I was enjoying it, I had no idea how much I was really going to need it that morning.

I literally expected to be at the studio for about an hour, maybe even less. But my new best friend and breakfast provider handed me a list of 12 interviews I'd be doing back to back, ending just before noon! In addition to the few leads I had given her, she had sold my story to a bunch of other stations across the country and Canada. Over the next several hours, I'd be broadcast live in Los Angeles, San Francisco, New York, Chicago, Boston, Atlanta, Saskatchewan and — get ready for this — even Des Moines, Iowa! As I realized what I'd be doing for the next four hours or so, I know I looked like a deer in the headlights.

I was shown into a small studio space with headphones, a comfortable chair and all the water I could drink. After the third straight interview, I asked the lady in the control room if she had it memorized yet. "Not quite," she replied. "But I'm sure I will after listening to it eight or nine more times." Under normal circumstances I would have thought that was pretty funny. I know she had no idea what I'd been going through in the last 24 hours or so, but if I had a bazooka it would have been locked and loaded at that control room!

I finally finished all the interviews and fortunately my voice hung in there the whole time. I had one more commitment with *Inside Edition* later that afternoon and I promised myself that I wouldn't accept another invitation from anyone. Not even Oprah Winfrey or David Letterman could get me on their shows if their lives depended on it!

Like a gift from heaven, the producer from *Inside Edition* called me and said that they weren't going to do the piece on me after all. I was so snake bit at that point that I thanked him very quickly for his call and hung up before he could change his mind.

In the world of chemistry the word entropy describes the state of disarray that all matter tries to attain. That's exactly how I felt during my time in the Big Apple as external forces attempted to pull me apart. I know I was only in New York for two days, but it literally felt like two weeks. All I wanted to do at that point was get home, and that would prove to be a whole new adventure in itself.

Planes, Trains & Automobiles

Like clockwork, the limousine arranged by NBC arrived at my hotel at precisely 4:15 p.m. on Tuesday, January 7. My driver was polite but quiet, which was just as well because I didn't feel like saying much. There's a first time for everything, I guess! I couldn't have been happier when the door closed and we started moving toward

LaGuardia. I knew in the future I'd look back fondly on my personal collection of New York minutes, but right then I was pretty raw.

All I really wanted was to get some dinner, because once again, I hadn't eaten anything since my breakfast at the radio studio. By the time I got back to my hotel and packed up, I really didn't have a lot of time to do much of anything except wait for my ride. I wish I had asked the driver to stop at a McDonald's as we were crawling at a snail's pace in rush hour traffic. At the time, I figured it would be easier just to wait until I got to the airport.

We pulled into LaGuardia at about 5:30 p.m., with plenty of time to make my 7:15 p.m. flight from New York to Des Moines. I started my check-in process at one of the self-serve kiosks, and got a strange message saying that I couldn't check in until 7:15 p.m.

Danger, Will Robinson! Danger!

I asked one of the ticket agents what the issue was, and she directed me to a line that looked like it was about 10.4 miles long. My stomach was not happy with me!

While I was waiting in line, I received a text message from my mother-in-law, who does volunteer work at the Des Moines International Airport. "Oooops!" was all it said, but I knew right then what was coming next. In the text that followed, she confirmed my suspicion that my flight had been canceled. It took everything I had to keep my cool, but I remembered the Serenity Prayer and accepted what I wasn't going to be able to change. But still, I just wanted to break down and cry!

When I finally got to the counter, I gave the lady my reservation number and she attacked the keyboard in front of her. Clickety-clack, clickety-clack! She told me that I was on the 7:15 flight the next day.

"In the morning?" I said hopefully.

"P.M.," she replied.

I explained to her that I was starting to have hallucinations of the movie, *Planes, Trains & Automobiles*. "Isn't there any way I can get home tonight?" I pleaded.

Clickety-clack. "There's a direct flight to Omaha that leaves at 8:30 tonight," she said.

Now, Omaha is about 135 miles from Des Moines. It wouldn't be a fun trip, but I could do it. And I really needed to get home. I promised Principal Kelley that I'd be in class on Wednesday morning. "Okay, go ahead and book it," I said at last.

I should have been faster on my feet, because of course the flight had already filled up. "You're number one stand-by," she said. I swear, if John Candy was still alive, I would have been looking around to see where he was!

"Thank you," I said.

"Have a good evening," she replied. "Next!"

I swallowed hard and raced toward the security line. If I got on the flight, I'd rent a car in Omaha and drive to Des Moines, which would get me home at about three o'clock in the morning. Oh well, it was the best I could do.

Fortunately, I got through security without being taken aside for a pat down, and all I could think about was getting my favorite McDonald's dinner, the Premium McWrap Chicken & Ranch (Grilled). I looked all around Terminal D, but for the life of me I couldn't find a McDonald's restaurant. I saw two pizza places, a coffee bar, a gourmet market and a burger joint called Taste of Pat LaFrieda, but no Golden Arches. If I had had the time, or an ounce of energy left inside me, I might have explored the whole airport and found the McDonald's in Terminal C, but it just wasn't practical given that my flight to Omaha was boarding and I had to be there if a seat opened up.

I'm now confessing to God, and to the entire world, that for the first time in 110 days I broke my McDonald's Diet while I was waiting to escape from New York. Instead of the chicken wrap that I craved, I bought a bag of cashews, an apple and a Diet Pepsi.

I landed in Omaha at about 1:00 a.m. and made my way over to the rental car area, where I overheard a guy saying that he was going to Des Moines.

"Hey, do you want to split the cost of the car and go together?" I offered, thinking that sharing the ride with someone might help me stay awake for the two-hour drive.

"Sure. That sounds great," he said.

We got the car and started heading east. I found out that my new friend was in the construction business, and we engaged in friendly conversation.

"What do you do?" he said at one point.

I told him that I was a high school science teacher, and I noticed that he had a smartphone with him. "Can you get the Internet on that phone?"

"Yeah."

"Why don't you Google John Cisna?"

"Okay." A few seconds later he looked up at me, then back down at his phone, then up at me once more, then down at his phone again, and then back up at me. "Oh my God! That's you!"

He watched a couple of my videos, and I told him all about the experiment and my adventures in New York.

"We've got to go to a McDonald's!" he exclaimed. There's one McDonald's restaurant off the highway between Omaha and Des Moines, about 45 minutes east of the Nebraska state line. We pulled off the highway to check it out, but unfortunately it was closed at the early hour we were traveling. You're kidding me, right?

Chapter 8: Going through a Phase — 2

"Don't stop 'til you get enough."
— Michael Jackson

It was good to finally be back in Iowa after my trip to New York, but things were different. After all the media attention I couldn't go anywhere without being referred to as "The McDonald's Guy." Everyone was very nice about it, but after a while it just wasn't as fun as it had all started out to be. It took me an hour just to do something simple like get milk at the grocery store, for example, and when I went to McDonald's the attention was even more overwhelming.

One night, as I was having dinner at the McDonald's in the town of Nevada, a very well-dressed man approached me.

"Are you that teacher in Colo doing the McDonald's experiment?" he asked.

"Yes," I replied.

This particular gentleman told me that he ate at McDonald's about 10 times a week, and that after seeing all the news stories about me he was paying more attention to the menu and choosing things that he normally wouldn't get. He kept talking about how great the experiment was, and how important it is to be proactive about your health, especially by making better food choices. He added how impressed he was that I was setting such a good example for my high school students.

I was feeling pretty good about myself, and then I asked him what he did for a living. "Oh, I'm the director of the funeral home here in town," he replied.

I said that it was very nice to meet him, but that I hoped I didn't run into him again at his place of business!

The Cisna Breakfast

As bizarre as all the attention can be at times, I truly am happy that I've been able to inspire people to change their eating habits and not feel quite as guilty as they used to about going to McDonald's and other fast food restaurants. Just the other day, the mother of one of the girls on the Colo-NESCO basketball team came up to me and told me she went to the Nevada McDonald's Drive-Thru and ordered the Cisna Breakfast.

"What did they do?" I asked.

"They asked me to repeat what I said, so I told them I wanted the Cisna Breakfast!"

"Then what happened?" I probed.

She told me that a voice came out of the loudspeaker and said, "Hold on a minute." A little while later, the voice came back and said, "Okay, that'll be two Egg White Delights, a Fruit & Maple Oatmeal and a 1% milk?"

My friend said she yelled, "That's it!" into the microphone, and pulled up to pay for her order.

Stuff like this has been happening all the time since I got back from New York, and I guess I'm continuing to bring it all on myself by doing more interviews and staying on the diet for another 90 days.

Move over, Arnold

The goal of Phase 2 is to see if I can get even healthier by increasing the intensity of the exercise I'm doing. I made the decision to do this about a week before the first 90-day cycle was over with. I emailed Kevin O'Brien and Jim Baker to see if they'd continue to pay for my meals. They wanted to help in any way they could, because they were excited by the results I had already achieved.

With their continued support, I asked my friend Brenda Baker if she'd put together a training program for me. Brenda is a fitness instructor and personal trainer who's married to one of the assistant baseball coaches at Ballard High School. I'm the head coach of the Ballard Bombers, which, unlike high school teams in most parts of the country, has its season in the summer months.

Brenda and her husband are part owners of an indoor hardball training facility called Athletes Advantage. It's a really cool place that used to be an old horse barn. Now it offers six fully retractable batting cages, two Iron Mike pitching machines, room for infield practice and a workout area with weights and cardio equipment. I conduct my private hitting lessons at this facility, and now it's where I've been doing my Phase 2 workouts.

Based on my age and weight, Brenda put together a program that incorporates core training, weight training and aerobic exercise. We usually meet on Mondays, Wednesdays and Fridays, and on Tuesdays and Thursdays I play basketball against the girls' basketball team in Colo. The weekends are technically my days off, but I manage to get some activity in by pitching balls to my hitting students.

My workouts with Brenda are intense but quick. They're dramatically different from the brisk walking I did during Phase 1, but I'm still in and out of the facility in about 45 minutes. Here's a typical week on my customized training program:

Phase 2 Sample Workouts

Monday

Warm up
   5–10 minutes

Strength Training
   Circuit 1:
   * Ball squats with dumbbells, 8–10 reps
   * Standing dumbbell shoulder presses, 8–10 reps
   * Stability ball rollouts, 10–12 reps
   Rest one minute and complete one more round

Circuit 2:
- Lunges with dumbbells, 8–10 reps each leg
- One-arm dumbbell rows, 8–10 reps each side
- Prone stability ball knee tucks, 10–12 reps

Rest one minute and complete one more round

Circuit 3:
- Pushups, 8–10 reps
- Stability ball back extensions, 10–12 reps
- Stability ball leg curls, 8–10 reps

Rest one minute and complete one more round

Cardio Training/Treadmill
- 5 minutes of light walking and jogging
- 60 seconds at increased pace, followed by 90 seconds of rest (Repeat 6 times)
- 5 minutes of easy jogging and walking

Stretching
Static stretches, focusing on all major muscle groups

Wednesday

Warm up
5–10 minutes

Strength Training
Circuit 1:
- Dumbbell chest presses, 8–10 reps
- Bodyweight rows with suspension strap, 8–10 reps
- Prone knee tucks with suspension strap, 8–10 reps

Rest one minute and complete one more round

Circuit 2:
- Dumbbell step-ups, 8–10 reps
- Pushups, 8–10 reps
- Stability ball abdominal crunches, 10–12 reps

Rest one minute and complete one more round

Circuit 3:
- Dumbbell walking lunges, 8–10 reps each leg
- Stability ball back extensions, 10–12 reps
- Stability ball supine torso rotations, 10–12 reps each side

Rest one minute and complete one more round

Cardio Training/Treadmill
- 5 minutes of light walking and jogging
- 30 seconds at increased pace, followed by 60 seconds of rest (Repeat 6 times)
- 5 minutes of easy jogging and walking

Stretching
Static stretches, focusing on all major muscle groups

Friday

Warm up
5–10 minutes

Strength Training
Circuit 1:
- Dumbbell single leg bench squats (rear foot on bench), 8–10 reps
- One-arm dumbbell rows, 8–10 reps each side
- Side crunches on stability ball, 10–12 reps each side

Rest one minute and complete one more round

Circuit 2:
- Pushups, 8–10 reps
- Assisted band pull-ups, 8–10 reps
- Stability ball squats, 8–10 reps

Rest one minute and complete one more round

Circuit 3:
- Kettlebell swings, 10–15 reps
- Standing dumbbell shoulder presses, 8–10 reps
- Cross body mountain climbers, 10–12 reps each side

Rest one minute and complete one more round

Cardio Training/Treadmill
- 5 minutes of light walking and jogging
- 45 seconds at increased pace, followed by 60 seconds of rest (Repeat 6 times)
- 5 minutes of easy jogging and walking

Stretching
Static stretches, focusing on all major muscle groups

What's Happening to Me?

The first phase of my experiment was meant to show the health impact of a 2,000-calorie-per-day McDonald's Diet on a regular person doing moderate exercise. The second phase is designed to find out the health impact of that same diet on a person doing higher intensity activity.

Let's start with my weight. When I began the whole experiment back in September of 2013, I tipped the scales at 280.2 pounds. By the end of the first 90 days, I was 37 pounds lighter, or 243 pounds. Halfway through Phase 2, I had dropped another 10 pounds to hit 233. And at the time of this writing — just two weeks before the end of Phase 2 — I'm weighing in at 224 pounds.

My current results have been telling me different things about the effectiveness of my new program. For one thing, I've managed to steadily keep losing weight for a longer time period than most people do when they start a diet and exercise program. Usually, people lose more weight in the beginning and then start to hit plateaus fairly quickly as their metabolism starts to compensate for the lack of food. But because I started out with moderate exercise and only increased my level of activity after the first 90 days, I was able to keep losing weight at a rapid pace for about 135 days straight.

Then I hit a plateau. Changes in my body were preventing me from losing weight, and I was stuck at 230 pounds for two weeks. Because I was exercising more strenuously but keeping my calories constant, my body thought it was starving and my metabolism slowed down to conserve energy. Brenda had me take a week off from the workouts we'd been doing together, and sure enough I started losing weight again.

I probably won't be able to lose weight as rapidly in the future unless I take more breaks from strenuous exercise and do more cardio training. I'm learning that dieting requires constant adjustments, and that some of the old rules no longer apply as my fitness level improves. My new workouts are helping me build muscle, for example. Muscle weighs more than fat, so my weight may stay the same or even increase even though I may continue to lose fat.

The good news is that I'm still losing inches, so I know that the fat is continuing to melt off. At the time of this writing, my stomach is down to 42 inches! I'm actually getting to the point where I'll have to start shopping for some new clothes. People have asked me whether or not I've had to buy a whole new wardrobe, but up until now that hasn't been the case.

As I've mentioned, I've battled with my weight for a very long time. About 10 years ago, I bit the bullet and forked over the cash to go to Jenny Craig. I got my weight down to about 230 pounds on that program, and had to buy a bunch of new suits and sport coats for business. They were so nice and styled so timelessly that I decided to hang onto them as I grew out of them over the past decade. They've definitely come in handy in the last few months, although I'll probably have to have them taken in or replace them with something new before too long.

Streamlined Meal Plans

I'm still using my daily McDonald's menus during this phase of the experiment, but I've simply been using my five favorite menus from Phase 1. I genuinely enjoy these particular menus, they fit my calorie target, and they come as close as can be expected to giving me 100 percent of the RDAs of the nutrient values we've been tracking since the beginning.

For your convenience, I'm including these five daily menus for you here. They include calorie counts for each menu item, plus a total calorie count for each day. (Please note that salad calorie counts include dressing.) If you want to get started on my McDonald's Diet right away, you can use these menus to take you through 90 days, 180 days or as long as you want to stay on it. Before you start this diet, please consult your doctor — and monitor your blood work every couple of months if you can.

Phase 2 Daily Menus

PHASE 2 DAILY MENU 1 — 2,000 Calories

Breakfast	Calories
Egg White Delight McMuffin	250
Hash Browns	150
Fruit & Maple Oatmeal	290
1% Low Fat Milk Jug	100

Lunch	
Premium Bacon Ranch Salad	180
Fruit 'N Yogurt Parfait	150
Apple Slices (2 bags)	30

Dinner	
Premium Grilled Chicken Classic Sandwich	350
Ranch Snack Wrap (Grilled)	270
World Famous Fries (small)	230
Large Diet Coke	0

PHASE 2 DAILY MENU 2 — 1,980 Calories

Breakfast	Calories
Egg White Delight McMuffin (2)	500
Fruit & Maple Oatmeal	290
Hash Browns	150
1% Low Fat Milk Jug	100

Lunch	
Premium Bacon Ranch Salad	180
Fruit 'N Yogurt Parfait	150
Apple Slices (2 bags)	30

Dinner	
Premium Grilled Chicken Classic Sandwich	350
World Famous Fries (small)	230
Large Diet Coke	0

PHASE 2 DAILY MENU 3 — 1,860 Calories

Breakfast	**Calories**
Egg White Delight McMuffin (2)	500
Fruit & Maple Oatmeal	290
Large Diet Coke	0

Lunch	
Premium Bacon Ranch Salad	180
Fruit 'N Yogurt Parfait	150

Dinner	
Premium McWrap Southwest (Grilled)	510
World Famous Fries (small)	230
Large Diet Coke	0

PHASE 2 DAILY MENU 4 — 1,770 Calories

Breakfast	Calories
Egg White Delight McMuffin (2)	500
Fruit & Maple Oatmeal	290
Large Diet Coke	0

Lunch	
Premium Bacon Ranch Salad	180
Fruit 'N Yogurt Parfait	150

Dinner	
Bacon Buffalo Ranch McChicken	420
World Famous Fries (small)	230
Large Diet Coke	0

PHASE 2 DAILY MENU 5 — 1,990 Calories

Breakfast	**Calories**
Egg White Delight McMuffin (2)	500
Hash Browns	150
1% Low Fat Milk Jug	100

Lunch	
Premium Grilled Chicken Ranch BLT Sandwich	440
Fruit 'N Yogurt Parfait	150
Large Diet Coke	0

Dinner	
Premium Caesar Salad with Grilled Chicken	230
Ranch Snack Wrap (Grilled)	270
Fruit 'N Yogurt Parfait	150
Large Diet Coke	0

These days, every time I go into the McDonald's in Nevada, Iowa, they're already putting my favorite breakfast and lunch together. By the time I get to the counter, they're handing me two Egg White Delights, a Fruit & Maple Oatmeal, a 1% Low Fat Milk Jug, a Premium Bacon Ranch Salad, a Fruit 'N Yogurt Parfait and two bags of Apple Slices. I've gotten to know most of the employees there quite well, and I really appreciate how supportive they've been.

And yes, each morning I still see the retired guys who gather at this McDonald's to shoot the breeze. They always ask me where in the world I'll be doing an interview next, and they keep me up to date on what's been written about me in the local newspapers. In return, I make sure they're eating their Egg White Delights!

One evening, I remember coming in for dinner and seeing them all there again. There was a large group of women at another set of tables, and I was wondering what was going on. I found out that the ladies were their wives, and that they've also remained a tight-knit group of friends over the years. What a super group of people they all are. I'm really going to miss going into that McDonald's every morning and starting my day off with them.

Tears, Sweat and Blood

While weight loss is certainly the most visible and talked about aspect of my McDonald's Diet, it's really not the most significant. I can't stress to you enough that the real question — the question of my overall health — can only be answered by my blood work.

If you remember, my lab results came out great at the end of the first 90 days, and I found myself moving out of the danger zone across the board. In Phase 2 of the experiment, my blood work was just as impressive. After nearly 180 days on my McDonald's Diet, I've stayed within acceptable ranges for cholesterol, triglycerides, glucose and salts.

Fig. 3

My McDonald's Diet Blood Work

	9/16/13	11/1/13	12/14/13	1/28/14	3/4/14
Total Cholesterol	249 mg/dL	189 mg/dL	170 mg/dL	194 mg/dL	190 mg/dL
LDL	170 mg/dL	129 mg/dL	113 mg/dL	132 mg/dL	128 mg/dL
Triglycerides	156 mg/dL	94 mg/dL	80 mg/dL	88 mg/dL	94 mg/dL
Chol/HDL	5.19:1	4.61:1	4.15:1	4.40:1	4.42:1

I can conclude from these results that my McDonald's Diet, combined with regular exercise of any intensity, can make an obese person considerably healthier. I know I'm just one person, but if I can do it, chances are pretty good that others — maybe even you — can do it too.

Chapter 9: What Choices Will You Make?

"Every choice you make has an end result."
— Zig Ziglar

I think the first choice I'll probably make when I complete Phase 2 of my McDonald's Diet will be to have a big dinner consisting of scallops, shrimp, asparagus and rice. It's what I've been missing the most during the past several months. But frankly, until I get to the end of Phase 2 I really don't know what I'll do next. I may continue eating at McDonald's. I may eat 2,000 calories a day in some other way. Or, although it's highly unlikely, I may even gain all my weight back! I know that whatever happens to me will be the result of the choices I make, and that's actually pretty empowering stuff.

Wherever we are today when it comes to our weight and our overall health — or really any other aspect of our lives, including careers, relationships, financial status, etc. — is the result of choices we've made. If we're not where we want to be, it's often because we haven't made the best choices. This experiment has shown me that it's never too late to make choices that can change your life for the better. I'm 55 years old, and the choice I made to eat nothing but McDonald's for breakfast, lunch and dinner for 90 days has gotten me on a path to better health and has given me a platform to make a difference in the lives of millions of people.

Doing this experiment has made me realize how much easier it is to make bad choices than it is to make good ones. The proof of this, at least when it comes to our health, is obvious in the overwhelming obesity statistics that I talked about in Chapter 1. As apparent — and as damaging — as the results of our society's bad food choices are, however, we've become quite good at ignoring them. Before I went on my McDonald's Diet I was as guilty as anyone of making bad choices for my body. Maybe it's because the results of those choices happened so gradually over time that I didn't even realize what I was doing to myself. Or maybe deep down I thought that my food choices were good ones because they gave me some immediate gratification, comfort or convenience. We can be deceived by the choices we make, and I was setting myself up to pay a potentially hefty price in the long run for some relatively insignificant short-term benefit.

The Compound Effect

My McDonald's Diet experiment opened my eyes to the significance of the decisions we make every day, and to how powerful even little changes in behavior can be over time. One thing that I've learned from my experiment is that our choices really don't have to be that dramatic to have dramatic results. I didn't become a vegan or an exercise fanatic during my experiment. I didn't deprive myself of foods that tasted good. I simply gave myself some calorie parameters and added a little bit of exercise into my life.

Darren Hardy, the publisher of *Success* magazine, calls this the "compound effect." In his best-selling book of the same name he explains how "Small, Smart Choices + Consistency + Time = RADICAL DIFFERENCE." He maintains that the power of the compound effect works for or against us every single day — whether we're conscious of it or not — because we're *always* making choices about something. What he tries to get us to do in his book is to deliberately make the kind of small choices that will help us, rather than unknowingly make choices that will be harmful.

His is a wake up call to excellence that shows us how close we really are to reaching and exceeding our potentials. "It takes very little extra to be EXTRAordinary," he writes. "In all areas of your life, look for the multiplier opportunities where you can go a little further, push yourself a little harder, last a little longer, prepare a little better, and deliver a little bit more. Where can you do better and more than expected? When can you do the totally unexpected? Find as many opportunities for "WOW," and the level and speed of your accomplishments will astonish you ... and everyone else around you." This guy would be a great high school teacher.

A Diet Plan for Real People

Initially, the only thing I set out to learn from my McDonald's Diet experiment was whether the hypothesis that an out-of-shape person could become healthier eating nothing but McDonald's for breakfast, lunch and dinner for 90 days straight was true or not.

I really didn't expect the results of my experiment to reach any farther than the Colo-NESCO Junior-Senior High School campus. But after the whole thing went viral, after reading thousands of emails, tweets, blog posts and letters, and after talking to random people at the grocery store, at the McDonald's I go to, and virtually everywhere else, it became quite apparent that my experiment has given lots of people hope in their desperate attempts to try to lose weight and get healthier.

Dietitians and nutritionists are a little bit cautious with me. On the one hand, they see the positive effects of what I've been doing. But on the other hand, they seem like they'd rather die before actually recommending that people eat fast food.

Registered dietitian and *TODAY* show contributor Joy Bauer, for example, who joined me on my segment with Matt Lauer and Savannah Guthrie, was squirming in her chair the whole time and kept saying that I would have felt a lot better if I did my same diet with no fast food. She wanted me to eat things like "vegetable omelets, lentil soups, fish with broccoli and sweet potato." But I felt great eating at McDonald's! Plus, I wanted to prove that regular people, who are on a budget or have busy schedules and kids running around, could do what I did.

Bauer also thought that most people wouldn't be able to follow my McDonald's Diet because the temptation to order too much at a fast food restaurant is just too great. She was buying into the myth, perpetrated by Morgan Spurlock's *Super Size Me*, that a person's will power is no match for the fast food industry and all its advertising dollars, beautiful photography and catchy slogans. Somehow I managed to overcome all the pressure, and I'm just a high school science teacher from Colo, Iowa!

Bauer got to the heart of the matter when she said, "I think what John proved is that it's not where you eat, it's what you eat." Of course, that's true. The choices we make are what make us fat, not McDonald's or any other food establishment. You can become fat at lots of restaurants and you can become healthy at lots of restaurants. The point is that the choices we make are what determine our state of health. And if we decide to make "small, smart choices" consistently over time, we're giving ourselves, and the people around us, a great gift.

You should understand by now that I'm not suggesting that you — or anyone else— spend the rest of your life eating nothing but McDonald's. However, and this is important, McDonald's can be a pathway to a healthier lifestyle. The vast majority of people can't afford to go to Weight Watchers or Jenny Craig. They can't afford to hire personal trainers. The vast majority of people don't have the luxury of time and money to follow a custom-made health plan.

Most people want meals that are affordable, quick and delicious. All three of these adjectives describe McDonald's food. And if I can convince the busy mom, the hard-working trucker, the on-the-go salesperson and countless others that they can still go to McDonald's and get healthier, then I'm really making a difference in the lives of real people.

This experiment of mine has given me the passion to tell people all around the world to stop using McDonald's and other fast food chains as scapegoats for their weight problems. I now know that after eating nearly 180 days of nothing but McDonald's that I can still eat a Big Mac or a Quarter Pounder and a side of fries if I want to. I just have to balance out the rest of my day, and be aware of my calorie intake in relation to the recommended daily allowances of different nutrients. This isn't rocket science, people!

Nor is it easy. I've battled weight problems all my life, and I think I can safely say that I'm a recovering foodaholic. It's a tough addiction, because you have to eat to stay alive and temptation is all around you. But to anyone reading this book having a hard time with his or her weight as I did, I can say with 100 percent certainty that this experiment offers a real opportunity to finally emerge victorious.

I've tried to make my McDonald's Diet as simple as possible, and I really do hope that the balanced menus at the end of this book will give you the motivation you need to become healthier. Maybe it's because I'm a science teacher, but I liked having guidelines for how much I could eat in a day. Before I set parameters for myself, it was a total free for all. But just like the studies I mentioned earlier — which proved that awareness of nutrition information leads people to make lower-calorie choices— sometimes a little understanding is all you need to get going.

The fact that I was able to lose weight — and get healthier — eating nothing but McDonald's means that you don't need a lot of health tips or gimmicks or "weird tricks" to lose weight. Improving your health comes down to two things — keeping your calories low and increasing your exercise. My McDonald's Diet is so simple that anyone can do it. Just eat about 2,000 calories a day and make adjustments, if needed, according to your individual calorie requirements. Add in 45 minutes of walking (or as much as you can) for four or five days a week, and slowly increase your activity level as you get comfortable working out.

That's really all there is to it! And once you're on your way to becoming healthy, whether it's by trying my McDonald's Diet for three months or just making adjustments in your current lifestyle, then you can design a more complete program for yourself that keeps you moving forward. Let me tell you, once you start seeing results, you'll get all kinds of attention and you'll be motivated to keep at it.

Patience Pays Off

The first six weeks of my experiment were the toughest for me for a variety of reasons. I missed eating the way I normally did. Everyone ridiculed what I was doing. And I was disappointed with myself for not being able to complete my goal of walking for 45 minutes straight right away. But I persisted and used the power of the compound effect to create significant changes in my life over time. I didn't push myself too hard with the exercise, for example. I simply added a little more time and covered a little more distance each day.

It seemed like great results came all of a sudden about six weeks into the program, but that wasn't true. The results came about because of all the work I did in the first 42 days. It was the compound effect in action! And when people started to say things like, "Wow, you're really doing it!" or "John, you're actually looking thinner!" or "Gosh, I was really wrong about this," I became more motivated to keep going. And at that point, it became less difficult partly because I had settled into the new routine, and partly because the improvements I was making in my body actually made the whole program somewhat enjoyable.

My point is that if you can hang in there for a month or so, if you can stay patient and focused while still eating an occasional Big Mac, then you'll be well on your way to success with this diet.

I really do hope that McDonald's and other fast food companies around the world will take advantage of my little experiment and build on the nutrition education they're already providing to consumers. Think of the impact that McDonald's and other restaurants could have in this country alone if they put together simple daily menus for people. I've already done that for you and they're all at the back of this book. Feel free to use them or make your own at the places where you like to eat!

The Inspirational Wall

I believe that people need something, or someone, to give them a reason to get up each morning. Everyone needs a purpose to make living each day a meaningful experience. Without a purpose, life can be empty and unsatisfying. That's how I felt when I was caught up in the corporate rat race, and it's why I was so sure that I wanted to return to teaching before I really was too old to do it. My faith guides me to learn and to love, and when it's my turn to be judged I want to be able to say that I've used my gifts to help people live better lives.

I always talk to people — especially my students — about the importance of being positive. When I first started teaching in Colo, there was a really ugly, blank green wall in my classroom. I asked the principal if I could put something on this wall, and he said I could do anything I wanted to it.

"Can I write on it?" I asked.

"You can do anything you want to it," he said again.

The next day, I took a red marker and wrote the words "Inspirational Wall" right in the center of this hideous structure. And off to the side I wrote down a quote: "The greatest failure is never to try."

When my kids came into class that morning, I told them that I wanted them to guess who said those inspirational words. "We're going to play 20 questions, and whoever gets the answer will get a Tootsie Roll," I announced.

My students asked me if the author of that quote was a man or a woman, a philosopher or a scientist, an actor or a writer — things like that. Everyone seemed to perk up a little bit and pay attention to what was going on. In the teaching profession we use the term "bell ringer" to describe an activity that can get kids into learning mode at the beginning of a class, and this was proving to be a very effective one.

It turns out that I got the exact quote wrong, but the person I was thinking of was Theodore Roosevelt. What he really said was, "It is hard to fail, but it is worse never to have tried to succeed." None of my students got the piece of candy that day, but my class had a great discussion of what the words I wrote down meant for our own lives.

My "Inspirational Wall" is the most powerful thing I've ever done as a teacher.

Every day since then I've been adding quotes to that wall. It now contains well over 300 great phrases, in indelible marker, from the most insightful and provocative people throughout history. Our little 20-questions game only takes about three or four minutes, but I believe it imparts valuable life lessons and really gets kids thinking. I know it's working because kids will often give me their own suggestions for quotes to put on the wall. I tell them that if I approve their quote, they get to lead the 20 questions.

The inspirational wall has been the most powerful thing I've ever done as a teacher because it helps kids realize that it's better to be positive than to let the negative things in life weigh you down. Everyone who knows me will tell you that I'm usually in a good mood. I work hard at it. Being positive in my interactions with my students, colleagues, friends, family members and even media personalities has served me well in my life, and I want everyone to reap the same rewards from positivity that I have.

Keeping a positive outlook on life helped me create and stick to my McDonald's Diet, and I hope that my story of weight loss under the Golden Arches inspires you to make positive changes in your own life. I'm living proof that something as farfetched as eating nothing but McDonald's for breakfast, lunch and dinner for 90 days — and then 90 more — can actually make a human being healthier. Take this information and run with it, and please let me know how it works for you. You can email me at John@MyMcDonaldsDietBook.com or follow me on Facebook at facebook.com/MyMcDonaldsDietBook.

See you at Mickey D's!

Epilogue

My McDonald's Diet has taken me places and introduced me to people I never thought I'd see. It's been a wild ride with unexpected results, and interest continues to grow as I make more media appearances and give more interviews.

Recently I was invited back on *Your World with Neil Cavuto* to comment on a plan to sue the fast food industry for making people fat. (You probably know where I landed on that issue: I think people make themselves fat.) And, as I write this, I'm getting ready for a new round of media visits to update my progress.

My three students and I have been invited to visit McDonald's headquarters and spend a day in Chicago. It's going to be especially exciting for the kids, who've never been on a plane before! My relationship with McDonald's is evolving, and I've also been asked to speak at several of their meetings and conferences in the months ahead.

A McDonald's franchisee in West Virginia invited me to help her educate people on how to live a healthy, balanced lifestyle. Her letter came to me on the heels of her state being named the fattest in the country. As an educator I look forward to my new role in helping adults, as well as children, make better nutritional choices and take control over their diets.

As the days unfold, I'm sure I'll have more information to provide you about food, nutrition, exercise and life in the spotlight. Please keep in touch with me at facebook.com/MyMcDonaldsDietBook and @johncisna on Twitter. I want to know what questions you have for me and I want to hear all about your McDonald's Diet experiences.

Acknowledgements

I didn't decide to write a book about my McDonald's Diet until after I got home from New York and had time to reflect on the whole experience. When I realized that so many people wanted to get their hands on my menus and get more details about my story, I thought that a book could be a real opportunity to make a difference in a lot of people's lives.

I had no idea how to even start a project like this, but fortunately I had a team of knowledgeable and experienced people to back me up. My former boss, Jon Brinton, put the wheels in motion, led the publishing team, and kept things moving at an incredibly aggressive pace. When he makes up his mind to do something, he really gets it done. He had the presence of mind to hire Dan Corredor to manage the project. Dan runs a creative marketing group in Phoenix, Arizona, called Asylum-Pipeline, and he stepped up to the plate big time. Dan handled all the day-to-day details, from developing cover concepts to arranging distribution. He's one of the most organized guys I know, and he kept everyone on schedule. I spent the majority of my time working on this project with someone Dan referred me to, a ghostwriter named Ed Sweet, who I immediately, and affectionately, nicknamed "Casper." Casper took the initial thoughts I had written down and conducted countless question-and-answer sessions with me to capture my voice and tell my story in an engaging way.

Author and editor Steven Beschloss provided invaluable guidance to sharpen the manuscript and help us prepare for publication. Editor Carol Harangody also added insights to make this a better book. Adrienne Silverman put her eagle eyes on the final manuscript for a proofread and a polish. Bob Diercksmeier of RJD Creative in Phoenix provided all manner of creative direction, and he and his team designed the book cover. John Johnson of J.J. Johnson Photo in Des Moines, Iowa, shot the cover photo and a lot of the other pictures you see inside this book. And the good people at Vook took all the components and turned them into an e-book in every possible file format, as well as the print edition you are holding in your hands right now. I owe a debt of gratitude to all of these artists for making my story come to life.

I will always be grateful to McDonald's franchisees Kevin O'Brien and Jim Baker for taking a chance on this wild idea of mine. This project would never have happened if they didn't believe in me and, more importantly, in the food they sell every day. Jim Baker has a terrific team at his McDonald's in Nevada, Iowa, and I want to thank them all — Shanna Blankenship, Stephanie Eichenberger, Heidi Fisher, Kellina Kuebler, Kyle Lehman, Kimberly Meyer, Greg Minor, Kathleen Murphy, Joe Roney, Amber Siefken, Rachel Vermeys and Kelsea Zimmerman — for serving me my meals and making me feel so welcome.

I have to also express my appreciation to my colleagues in the Colo-NESCO school district. To the administration, led by superintendent Jim Verlengia and principal Brandon Kelley, thank you for letting me play hooky so I could do interviews and make speeches. To my fellow faculty members — including Dana Accola, Jackie Dunlap, Priscilla Gammon and Josh Nessa — thank you for all the good-natured teasing, your willingness to be videotaped and your ultimate support once you realized that this crazy idea was actually working.

Tanner Clatt, Savannah Deupree and Grant Tiarks, my student cohorts in this experiment, I couldn't have done this without your help. Thank you for the daily menus and for tolerating the many meetings and sidebar conversations we had throughout the 90 days of this experiment. I know the work wasn't easy, but I hope you'll see how it will help prepare you for life in the real world as you pursue your dreams.

While these three particular students played a pivotal role in conducting the experiment, all the other students on campus were involved and I want to thank them, as well. As the story unfolded, especially after it went viral, it was fun to watch the level of excitement that spread throughout the school. Specific thanks go to the kids who gave their honest opinions of me in my documentary video, including Shelby Anthony, Clayton Bryan, Morgan Dunahoo, Devin Francis, Jillian Gibbons, Ricki Grover, Peyton Hall, Jacob Hapes, Brooke Hunter, Olivia Key, Zoee Risdal and Michael Starling.

This book wouldn't be possible if media professionals and personalities around the world didn't think my story had any legs. I thank all of them for taking an interest in what I was doing, particularly my friend Kevin Cooney, main anchorman at KCCI in Des Moines. He referred my story to reporter Mark Tauscheck, who, during a regular eight-hour shift that included two hours of travel time, put together the amazing piece that started the whole thing rolling. Mark is a great guy, and we've become quite close as a result of our connection.

I also want to thank Alicyn Hanford from United Stations Radio Network for saving my life in New York, and Neil Cavuto for taking time to write me a thank-you note for appearing on his show, and for agreeing to write the foreword for this book.

A very big supporter for me personally from day one was Anne Sullivan, my wife's best friend who introduced me to Kevin O'Brien. Anne is the chief of human resources for the Des Moines public school system, and she shares my commitment to helping students excel. She was also committed to helping me excel, and her continued cheerleading of my weight loss and health gain resonated throughout the experiment. I'm very grateful for her support and friendship during this time.

Most of all, I want to express my love and gratitude to my wife and daughters. Dani, Jamie and Laura are the lights of my life. And Kim, who's stuck by me and supported me in all my ventures good and bad for the past 37 years, is my true source of strength. There just aren't words that can adequately express how thankful I am to have her in my life.

Bonus Section: My McDonald's Diet Daily Menus

For those of you who want to follow my McDonald's Diet, here are all the unique daily menus from the original experiment. Please note that there are fewer than 90 of them because we repeated certain menus throughout the program. Use the planning guide at the end of this section to see which menu I used on each day.

My nutritional targets were based on a 2,000-calorie-per-day diet. If you've ever read a Nutrition Facts label, you know that this is our national standard. The number was a compromise solution chosen to avoid having to put too much information on those labels. In actuality, USDA food consumption surveys showed that men typically consume 2,000 to 3,000 calories per day, women 1,600 to 2,200, and children 1,800 to 2,500. For this reason, you'll also notice another line on the Nutrition Facts Label: "Your daily values may be higher or lower depending on your calorie needs."

I encourage most men and women to start with the menus included here, because they also reflect our efforts to get other nutritional values as close as possible to 100 percent of the RDA. Keep in mind that your specific calorie requirements are based on numerous factors, including age, gender, activity level and life stage. But one thing is true for all of us. If you're eating too many calories, you're going to gain weight. I knew that 2,000 calories a day was less than my body needed to sustain itself at 280 pounds, so I knew that I'd lose weight on this diet.

My daily calorie target was 2,000 per day, but you'll notice that some menus go a little over that and some menus are under the target. We made adjustments to keep my average daily calorie count as close to 2,000 as we could throughout the experiment, and you'll likely have to do the same. To help you, I've also indicated the calories for each item on the daily menus. And I encourage you to use the Meal Builder function at mcdonalds.com to calculate nutritional values if you decide to follow this diet at McDonald's. Please note that the calorie counts listed in my daily menus for salads include dressing. (On the McDonald's website the calorie counts for salads are given without dressing.)

I ate three meals a day for convenience, but there's no reason why you couldn't spread out your total number of daily calories across four, five or even six mini-meals. Many dietitians believe that "grazing" throughout the day encourages additional weight loss because it keeps your metabolism elevated.

My recommendation is to keep things as simple as you can in the beginning, and then make adjustments as you go. You don't really need any tricks or gimmicks with this diet — just keep your calories and nutrients close to recommended daily amounts and try to get some moderate exercise four or five days a week.

One more thing: You'll notice that I typically ordered a drink at breakfast and another at dinner. Throughout each day, I'd also enjoy unsweetened iced tea and keep myself hydrated with plenty of water.

DAILY MENU 1 — 2,080 Calories

Breakfast	Calories
Sausage Burrito	300
Fruit & Maple Oatmeal	290
Minute Maid® Premium Orange Juice	150

Lunch	
Premium Southwest Salad	230
Fruit 'N Yogurt Parfait	150
Apple Slices (2 bags)	30

Dinner	
Premium Grilled Chicken Classic Sandwich	350
Honey Mustard Snack Wrap (Grilled)	250
Hot Fudge Sundae	330
Large Diet Coke®	0

DAILY MENU 2 — 2,055 Calories

Breakfast	Calories
Sausage Burrito (2)	600
Minute Maid® Premium Orange Juice	150

Lunch	
Premium Bacon Ranch Salad	180
Fruit 'N Yogurt Parfait	150
Apple Slices (1 bag)	15

Dinner	
Double Cheeseburger	440
Vanilla Reduced Fat Ice Cream Cone	170
Large Diet Coke®	0

DAILY MENU 3 — 2,045 Calories

Breakfast	Calories
Sausage Burrito	300
Fruit & Maple Oatmeal	290
Minute Maid® Premium Orange Juice	150

Lunch	
Premium Southwest Salad	230
Fruit 'N Yogurt Parfait	150
Apple Slices (1 bag)	15

Dinner	
Premium Grilled Chicken Classic Sandwich	350
World Famous Fries (small)	230
Hot Fudge Sundae	330
Large Diet Coke	0

DAILY MENU 4 — 1,925 Calories

Breakfast	Calories
Sausage Burrito	300
Fruit & Maple Oatmeal	290
Minute Maid® Premium Orange Juice	150

Lunch	
Fruit 'N Yogurt Parfait	150
Apple Slices (1 bag)	15

Dinner	
Premium Grilled Chicken Classic Sandwich	350
Double Cheeseburger	440
World Famous Fries (small)	230
Large Diet Coke	0

DAILY MENU 5 — 2,100 Calories

Breakfast	Calories
Sausage Burrito	300
Fruit & Maple Oatmeal	290
Minute Maid® Premium Orange Juice	150

Lunch	
Premium McWrap Chicken & Bacon (Grilled)	460
Fruit 'N Yogurt Parfait	150
Large Diet Coke	0

Dinner	
Premium Grilled Chicken Classic Sandwich	350
World Famous Fries (small)	330
Vanilla Reduced Fat Ice Cream Cone	170
Large Diet Coke	0

DAILY MENU 6 — 2,050 Calories

Breakfast	Calories
Sausage Burrito	300
Fruit & Maple Oatmeal	290
Minute Maid® Premium Orange Juice	150

Lunch	
Premium McWrap Chicken & Bacon (Grilled)	460
Premium Bacon Ranch Salad	180
Fruit 'N Yogurt Parfait	150

Dinner	
Premium Grilled Chicken Classic Sandwich	350
Vanilla Reduced Fat Ice Cream Cone	170
Large Diet Coke	0

DAILY MENU 7 — 2,080 Calories

Breakfast	Calories
Sausage Burrito	300
Fruit & Maple Oatmeal	290
Minute Maid® Premium Orange Juice	150

Lunch	
Premium Southwest Salad	230
Fruit 'N Yogurt Parfait	150
Apple Slices (2 bags)	30

Dinner	
Premium Grilled Chicken Classic Sandwich (2)	700
World Famous Fries (small)	230
Large Diet Coke	0

DAILY MENU 8 — 2,155 Calories

Breakfast	Calories
Sausage Burrito	300
Fruit & Maple Oatmeal	290
Minute Maid® Premium Orange Juice	150

Lunch	
Premium Southwest Salad	230
Fruit 'N Yogurt Parfait	150
Apple Slices (1 bag)	15

Dinner	
Premium Grilled Chicken Classic Sandwich	350
Double Cheeseburger	440
Premium Bacon Ranch Salad with Grilled Chicken	230
Large Diet Coke	0

DAILY MENU 9 — 1,730 Calories

Breakfast	Calories
Egg McMuffin	300
Fruit & Maple Oatmeal	290
Minute Maid® Premium Orange Juice	150

Lunch	
Premium Southwest Salad	230
Fruit 'N Yogurt Parfait	150
Apple Slices (2 bags)	30

Dinner	
Premium Grilled Chicken Classic Sandwich	350
Premium Bacon Ranch Salad with Grilled Chicken	230
Large Diet Coke	0

DAILY MENU 10 — 1,905 Calories

Breakfast	Calories
Egg McMuffin	300
Hash Browns	150
Fruit & Maple Oatmeal	290
Minute Maid® Premium Orange Juice	150

Lunch	
Premium Southwest Salad	230
Fruit 'N Yogurt Parfait	150
Apple Slices (1 bag)	15

Dinner	
Premium Grilled Chicken Classic Sandwich	350
Ranch Snack Wrap (Grilled)	270
Large Diet Coke	0

DAILY MENU 11 — 1,915 Calories

Breakfast	Calories
Egg McMuffin (2)	600
Hash Browns	150
Minute Maid® Premium Orange Juice	150

Lunch	
Premium Southwest Salad	230
Fruit 'N Yogurt Parfait	150
Apple Slices (1 bag)	15

Dinner	
Premium Grilled Chicken Classic Sandwich	350
Ranch Snack Wrap (Grilled)	270
Large Diet Coke	0

DAILY MENU 12 — 2,135 Calories

Breakfast	Calories
Egg McMuffin	300
Hash Browns	150
Fruit & Maple Oatmeal	290
Minute Maid® Premium Orange Juice	150

Lunch	
Premium Southwest Salad	230
Fruit 'N Yogurt Parfait	150
Apple Slices (1 bag)	15

Dinner	
Premium Grilled Chicken Classic Sandwich	350
Ranch Snack Wrap (Grilled)	270
World Famous Fries (small)	230
Large Diet Coke	0

DAILY MENU 13 — 2,120 Calories

Breakfast	Calories
Egg McMuffin	300
Hash Browns	150
Fruit & Maple Oatmeal	290
Minute Maid® Premium Orange Juice	150

Lunch	
Ranch Snack Wrap (Grilled)	270
Premium Southwest Salad	230
Fruit 'N Yogurt Parfait	150

Dinner	
Premium Grilled Chicken Classic Sandwich	350
World Famous Fries (small)	230
Large Diet Coke	0

DAILY MENU 14 — 2,000 Calories

Breakfast	Calories
Egg White Delight McMuffin	250
Hash Browns	150
Fruit & Maple Oatmeal	290
1% Low Fat Milk Jug	100

Lunch	
Premium Bacon Ranch Salad	180
Fruit 'N Yogurt Parfait	150
Apple Slices (2 bags)	30

Dinner	
Premium Grilled Chicken Classic Sandwich	350
Ranch Snack Wrap (Grilled)	270
World Famous Fries (small)	230
Large Diet Coke	0

DAILY MENU 15 — 1,995 Calories

Breakfast	Calories
Egg White Delight McMuffin	250
Hash Browns	150
Fruit & Maple Oatmeal	290
1% Low Fat Milk Jug	100

Lunch	
Premium Bacon Ranch Salad	180
Fruit 'N Yogurt Parfait	150
Apple Slices (1 bag)	15

Dinner	
Premium Grilled Chicken Classic Sandwich	350
6-piece Chicken McNuggets	280
World Famous Fries (small)	230
Large Diet Coke	0

DAILY MENU 16 — 1,945 Calories

Breakfast	Calories
Egg White Delight McMuffin (2)	500
Fruit & Maple Oatmeal	290
Large Diet Coke	0

Lunch	
Premium Southwest Salad	230
Fruit 'N Yogurt Parfait	150
Apple Slices (1 bag)	15

Dinner	
Cheeseburger	300
Premium Caesar Salad with Grilled Chicken	230
World Famous Fries (small)	230
Large Diet Coke	0

DAILY MENU 17 — 2,000 Calories

Breakfast	Calories
Egg White Delight McMuffin (2)	500
Fruit & Maple Oatmeal	290
Large Diet Coke	0

Lunch	
Premium Southwest Salad	230
Fruit 'N Yogurt Parfait	150

Dinner	
Premium Grilled Chicken Classic Sandwich	350
Premium Caesar Salad with Grilled Chicken	230
Baked Apple Pie	250
Large Diet Coke	0

DAILY MENU 18 — 2,000 Calories

Breakfast	Calories
Egg White Delight McMuffin	250
Sausage Burrito	300
Fruit & Maple Oatmeal w/out Brown Sugar	260
Large Diet Coke	0

Lunch	
Premium Southwest Salad	230
Fruit 'N Yogurt Parfait	150

Dinner	
Premium Grilled Chicken Classic Sandwich	350
Premium Caesar Salad with Grilled Chicken	230
World Famous Fries (small)	230
Large Diet Coke	0

DAILY MENU 19 — 2,020 Calories

Breakfast	Calories
Egg White Delight McMuffin (2)	500
Sausage Burrito	300
Fruit & Maple Oatmeal w/out Brown Sugar	260
Large Diet Coke	0

Lunch	
Premium Southwest Salad	230
Fruit 'N Yogurt Parfait	150

Dinner	
Premium Grilled Chicken Classic Sandwich	350
Premium Caesar Salad with Grilled Chicken	230
Large Diet Coke	0

DAILY MENU 20 — 2,010 Calories

Breakfast	Calories
Egg White Delight McMuffin	250
Hash Browns	150
Fruit & Maple Oatmeal	290
1% Low Fat Milk Jug	100

Lunch	
Premium Bacon Ranch Salad	180
Fruit 'N Yogurt Parfait	150
Apple Slices (2 bags)	30

Dinner	
Premium Grilled Chicken Classic Sandwich	350
6-piece Chicken McNuggets	280
World Famous Fries (small)	230
Large Diet Coke	0

DAILY MENU 21 — 1,960 Calories

Breakfast	Calories
Egg White Delight McMuffin (2)	500
Fruit & Maple Oatmeal	290
Large Diet Coke	0

Lunch	
Premium Southwest Salad	230
Fruit 'N Yogurt Parfait	150
Apple Slices (2 bags)	30

Dinner	
Cheeseburger	300
Premium Caesar Salad with Grilled Chicken	230
World Famous Fries (small)	230
Large Diet Coke	0

DAILY MENU 22 — 1,950 Calories

Breakfast	Calories
Egg White Delight McMuffin	250
Hash Browns	150
Fruit & Maple Oatmeal	290
Large Diet Coke	0

Lunch	
Premium Bacon Ranch Salad	180
Fruit 'N Yogurt Parfait	150
Apple Slices (2 bags)	30

Dinner	
Premium McWrap Chicken & Ranch (Grilled)	420
World Famous Fries (medium)	380
Large Diet Coke	0

DAILY MENU 23 — 2,000 Calories

Breakfast	Calories
Egg White Delight McMuffin	250
Sausage Burrito	300
Fruit & Maple Oatmeal	290
1% Low Fat Milk Jug	100

Lunch	
Premium Bacon Ranch Salad	180
Apple Slices (2 bags)	30

Dinner	
Premium Grilled Chicken Classic Sandwich	350
Ranch Snack Wrap (Grilled)	270
World Famous Fries (small)	230
Large Diet Coke	0

DAILY MENU 24 — 1,980 Calories

Breakfast	Calories
Egg White Delight McMuffin (2)	500
Fruit & Maple Oatmeal	290
Large Diet Coke	0

Lunch	
Premium Southwest Salad	230
Fruit 'N Yogurt Parfait	150

Dinner	
Premium Grilled Chicken Classic Sandwich	350
Premium Caesar Salad with Grilled Chicken	230
World Famous Fries (small)	230
Large Diet Coke	0

DAILY MENU 25 — 2,010 Calories

Breakfast	Calories
Egg White Delight McMuffin	250
Fruit & Maple Oatmeal	290
Hash Browns	150
1% Low Fat Milk Jug	100

Lunch	
Premium Bacon Ranch Salad	180
Fruit 'N Yogurt Parfait	150
Apple Slices (2 bags)	30

Dinner	
Premium Grilled Chicken Classic Sandwich	350
6-piece Chicken McNuggets	280
World Famous Fries (small)	230
Large Diet Coke	0

DAILY MENU 26 — 1,960 Calories

Breakfast	Calories
Egg White Delight McMuffin	250
Fruit & Maple Oatmeal	290
Hash Browns	150
1% Low Fat Milk Jug	100

Lunch	
Premium Bacon Ranch Salad	180
Fruit 'N Yogurt Parfait	150
Apple Slices (2 bags)	30

Dinner	
Premium Grilled Chicken Classic Sandwich	350
Premium Caesar Salad with Grilled Chicken	230
World Famous Fries (small)	230
Large Diet Coke	0

DAILY MENU 27 — 1,980 Calories

Breakfast	Calories
Egg White Delight McMuffin (2)	500
Fruit & Maple Oatmeal	290
Hash Browns	150
1% Low Fat Milk Jug	100

Lunch	
Premium Bacon Ranch Salad	180
Fruit 'N Yogurt Parfait	150
Apple Slices (2 bags)	30

Dinner	
Premium Grilled Chicken Classic Sandwich	350
World Famous Fries (small)	230
Large Diet Coke	0

DAILY MENU 28 — 1,590 Calories

Breakfast	Calories
Egg White Delight McMuffin (2)	500
Fruit & Maple Oatmeal	290
Large Diet Coke	0

Lunch	
Fruit 'N Yogurt Parfait	150
Large Diet Coke	0

Dinner	
Premium McWrap Chicken & Ranch (Grilled)	420
Premium Caesar Salad with Grilled Chicken	230
Large Diet Coke	0

DAILY MENU 29 — 1,880 Calories

Breakfast	Calories
Egg White Delight McMuffin (2)	500
Fruit & Maple Oatmeal	290
1% Low Fat Milk Jug	100

Lunch	
Fruit 'N Yogurt Parfait	150
Apple Slices (2 bags)	30

Dinner	
Premium Grilled Chicken Classic Sandwich	350
Premium Caesar Salad with Grilled Chicken	230
World Famous Fries (small)	230
Large Diet Coke	0

DAILY MENU 30 — 2,030 Calories

Breakfast	Calories
Egg White Delight McMuffin	250
Sausage Burrito	300
Fruit & Maple Oatmeal	290
Large Diet Coke	0

Lunch	
Premium Southwest Salad	230
Fruit 'N Yogurt Parfait	150

Dinner	
Premium Grilled Chicken Classic Sandwich	350
Premium Caesar Salad with Grilled Chicken	230
World Famous Fries (small)	230
Large Diet Coke	0

DAILY MENU 31 — 1,995 Calories

Breakfast	Calories
Egg White Delight McMuffin	250
Hash Browns (2)	300
Fruit & Maple Oatmeal	290
Large Diet Coke	0

Lunch	
Premium Bacon Ranch Salad	180
Fruit 'N Yogurt Parfait	150
Apple Slices (1 bag)	15

Dinner	
Premium Grilled Chicken Classic Sandwich	350
Premium Caesar Salad with Grilled Chicken	230
World Famous Fries (small)	230
Large Diet Coke	0

DAILY MENU 32 — 1,980 Calories

Breakfast	Calories
Egg White Delight McMuffin	250
Hash Browns (2)	300
Fruit & Maple Oatmeal	290
Large Diet Coke	0

Lunch	
Premium Bacon Ranch Salad	180
Fruit 'N Yogurt Parfait	150

Dinner	
Premium Grilled Chicken Classic Sandwich	350
Premium Caesar Salad with Grilled Chicken	230
World Famous Fries (small)	230
Large Diet Coke	0

DAILY MENU 33 — 1,865 Calories

Breakfast	Calories
Egg White Delight McMuffin (2)	500
Hash Browns	150
1% Low Fat Milk Jug	100

Lunch	
Premium Bacon Ranch Salad	180
Fruit 'N Yogurt Parfait	150
Apple Slices (1 bag)	15

Dinner	
Premium Grilled Chicken Classic Sandwich	350
Premium McWrap Chicken & Ranch (Grilled)	420
Large Diet Coke	0

DAILY MENU 34 — 2,020 Calories

Breakfast	Calories
Egg White Delight McMuffin	250
Hash Browns	150
Fruit & Maple Oatmeal	290
1% Low Fat Milk Jug	100

Lunch	
Premium Grilled Chicken Ranch BLT Sandwich	440
Premium Bacon Ranch Salad	180
Large Diet Coke	0

Dinner	
Premium Caesar Salad with Grilled Chicken	230
World Famous Fries (small)	230
Fruit 'N Yogurt Parfait	150
Large Diet Coke	0

DAILY MENU 35 — 1,990 Calories

Breakfast	Calories
Egg White Delight McMuffin (2)	500
Hash Browns	150
1% Low Fat Milk Jug	100

Lunch	
Premium Grilled Chicken Ranch BLT Sandwich	440
Fruit 'N Yogurt Parfait	150
Large Diet Coke	0

Dinner	
Premium Caesar Salad with Grilled Chicken	230
Ranch Snack Wrap (Grilled)	270
Fruit 'N Yogurt Parfait	150
Large Diet Coke	0

DAILY MENU 36 — 1,950 Calories

Breakfast	Calories
Egg White Delight McMuffin (2)	500
Hash Browns	150
1% Low Fat Milk Jug	100

Lunch	
Premium Grilled Chicken Ranch BLT Sandwich	440
Fruit 'N Yogurt Parfait	150
Large Diet Coke	0

Dinner	
Premium Caesar Salad with Grilled Chicken	230
World Famous Fries (small)	230
Fruit 'N Yogurt Parfait	150
Large Diet Coke	0

DAILY MENU 37 — 1,995 Calories

Breakfast	Calories
Egg White Delight McMuffin (2)	500
Fruit & Maple Oatmeal	290
Large Diet Coke	0

Lunch	
Premium Southwest Salad	230
Fruit 'N Yogurt Parfait	150
Apple Slices (1 bag)	15

Dinner	
Premium Grilled Chicken Classic Sandwich	350
Premium Caesar Salad with Grilled Chicken	230
World Famous Fries (small)	230
Large Diet Coke	0

DAILY MENU 38 — 1,980 Calories

Breakfast	Calories
Egg White Delight McMuffin (2)	500
Fruit & Maple Oatmeal	290
Hash Browns	150
1% Low Fat Milk Jug	100

Lunch	
Premium Bacon Ranch Salad	180
Fruit 'N Yogurt Parfait	150
Apple Slices (2 bags)	30

Dinner	
Premium Grilled Chicken Classic Sandwich	350
Premium Caesar Salad with Grilled Chicken	230
Large Diet Coke	0

DAILY MENU 39 — 1,400 Calories

Breakfast	Calories
Egg White Delight McMuffin	250
Hash Browns	150
Fat Free Chocolate Milk Jug	130

Lunch	
Premium Bacon Ranch Salad	180
Fruit 'N Yogurt Parfait	150

Dinner	
Deluxe Quarter Pounder	540
Large Diet Coke	0

DAILY MENU 40 — 1,750 Calories

Breakfast	Calories
Egg White Delight McMuffin (2)	500
Fruit & Maple Oatmeal	290
Large Diet Coke	0

Lunch	
Premium Southwest Salad	230
Fruit 'N Yogurt Parfait	150
Apple Slices (2 bags)	30

Dinner	
Big Mac	550
Large Diet Coke	0

DAILY MENU 41 — 1,640 Calories

Breakfast	Calories
Egg White Delight McMuffin	250
Fruit & Maple Oatmeal	290
Large Diet Coke	0

Lunch	
Fruit 'N Yogurt Parfait (2)	300
Apple Slices (2 bags)	30

Dinner	
Deluxe Quarter Pounder	540
World Famous Fries (small)	230
Large Diet Coke	0

DAILY MENU 42 — 1,620 Calories

Breakfast	Calories
Egg White Delight McMuffin	250
Fruit & Maple Oatmeal	290
Large Diet Coke	0

Lunch	
Premium Southwest Salad	230
Fruit 'N Yogurt Parfait	150
Apple Slices (2 bags)	30

Dinner	
Double Cheeseburger	440
World Famous Fries (small)	230
Large Diet Coke	0

DAILY MENU 43 — 1,790 Calories

Breakfast	Calories
Egg White Delight McMuffin (2)	500
Hash Browns	150
Large Diet Coke	0

Lunch	
Fruit & Maple Oatmeal	290
Fruit 'N Yogurt Parfait	150
Apple Slices (2 bags)	30

Dinner	
Daily Double	440
World Famous Fries (small)	230
Large Diet Coke	0

DAILY MENU 44 — 1,860 Calories

Breakfast	**Calories**
Egg White Delight McMuffin (2)	500
Fruit & Maple Oatmeal	290
Large Diet Coke	0

Lunch	
Premium Bacon Ranch Salad	180
Fruit 'N Yogurt Parfait	150

Dinner	
Premium Grilled Chicken Club Sandwich	510
World Famous Fries (small)	230
Large Diet Coke	0

DAILY MENU 45 — 1,710 Calories

Breakfast	Calories
Egg White Delight McMuffin	250
Fruit & Maple Oatmeal	290
Large Diet Coke	0

Lunch	
Fruit & Maple Oatmeal	290
Fruit 'N Yogurt Parfait	150

Dinner	
McRib	500
World Famous Fries (small)	230
Large Diet Coke	0

DAILY MENU 46 — 1,770 Calories

Breakfast	Calories
Egg White Delight McMuffin (2)	500
Fruit & Maple Oatmeal	290
Large Diet Coke	0

Lunch	
Premium Bacon Ranch Salad	180
Fruit 'N Yogurt Parfait	150

Dinner	
Bacon Buffalo Ranch McChicken	420
World Famous Fries (small)	230
Large Diet Coke	0

DAILY MENU 47 — 1,760 Calories

Breakfast	Calories
Egg White Delight McMuffin	250
Fruit & Maple Oatmeal	290
Large Diet Coke	0

Lunch	
Premium Southwest Salad	230
Fruit 'N Yogurt Parfait	150

Dinner	
Bacon Habanero Ranch Quarter Pounder	610
World Famous Fries (small)	230
Large Diet Coke	0

DAILY MENU 48 — 1,530 Calories

Breakfast	Calories
Egg White Delight McMuffin	250
Fruit & Maple Oatmeal	290
Large Diet Coke	0

Lunch	
Premium Bacon Ranch Salad	180
Fruit 'N Yogurt Parfait	150
Apple Slices (2 bags)	30

Dinner	
Bacon & Cheese Quarter Pounder	600
Apple Slices (2 bags)	30
Large Diet Coke	0

DAILY MENU 49 — 1,740 Calories

Breakfast	Calories
Egg White Delight McMuffin (2)	500
Fruit & Maple Oatmeal	290
Large Diet Coke	0

Lunch	
Premium Bacon Ranch Salad	180
Fruit 'N Yogurt Parfait	150

Dinner	
Filet-O-Fish	390
World Famous Fries (small)	230
Large Diet Coke	0

DAILY MENU 50 — 1,860 Calories

Breakfast	Calories
Egg White Delight McMuffin (2)	500
Fruit & Maple Oatmeal	290
Large Diet Coke	0

Lunch	
Premium Bacon Ranch Salad	180
Fruit 'N Yogurt Parfait	150

Dinner	
Premium McWrap Southwest (Grilled)	510
World Famous Fries (small)	230
Large Diet Coke	0

DAILY MENU 51 — 1,710 Calories

Breakfast	Calories
Egg White Delight McMuffin (2)	500
Fruit & Maple Oatmeal	290
Large Diet Coke	0

Lunch	
Premium Bacon Ranch Salad	180
Fruit 'N Yogurt Parfait	150

Dinner	
Premium McWrap Sweet Chili Chicken (Grilled)	360
World Famous Fries (small)	230
Large Diet Coke	0

DAILY MENU 52 — 1,700 Calories

Breakfast	Calories
Egg White Delight McMuffin (2)	500
Fruit & Maple Oatmeal	290
Large Diet Coke	0

Lunch	
Premium Bacon Ranch Salad	180
Fruit 'N Yogurt Parfait	150

Dinner	
Premium Grilled Chicken Classic Sandwich	350
World Famous Fries (small)	230
Large Diet Coke	0

My McDonald's Diet Planning Guide

Day 1 Daily Menu 1	**Day 16** Daily Menu 14	**Day 31** Daily Menu 21	**Day 46** Daily Menu 25	**Day 61** Daily Menu 33	**Day 76** Daily Menu 51
Day 2 Daily Menu 1	**Day 17** Daily Menu 14	**Day 32** Daily Menu 22	**Day 47** Daily Menu 21	**Day 62** Daily Menu 28	**Day 77** Daily Menu 52
Day 3 Daily Menu 2	**Day 18** Daily Menu 14	**Day 33** Daily Menu 17	**Day 48** Daily Menu 29	**Day 63** Daily Menu 34	**Day 78** Daily Menu 52
Day 4 Daily Menu 3	**Day 19** Daily Menu 14	**Day 34** Daily Menu 23	**Day 49** Daily Menu 30	**Day 64** Daily Menu 40	**Day 79** Daily Menu 51
Day 5 Daily Menu 4	**Day 20** Daily Menu 14	**Day 35** Daily Menu 18	**Day 50** Daily Menu 31	**Day 65** Daily Menu 41	**Day 80** Daily Menu 52
Day 6 Daily Menu 5	**Day 21** Daily Menu 14	**Day 36** Daily Menu 24	**Day 51** Daily Menu 32	**Day 66** Daily Menu 42	**Day 81** Daily Menu 33
Day 7 Daily Menu 6	**Day 22** Daily Menu 15	**Day 37** Daily Menu 25	**Day 52** Daily Menu 30	**Day 67** Daily Menu 43	**Day 82** Daily Menu 14
Day 8 Daily Menu 7	**Day 23** Daily Menu 15	**Day 38** Daily Menu 21	**Day 53** Daily Menu 33	**Day 68** Daily Menu 44	**Day 83** Daily Menu 14
Day 9 Daily Menu 8	**Day 24** Daily Menu 16	**Day 39** Daily Menu 26	**Day 54** Daily Menu 34	**Day 69** Daily Menu 45	**Day 84** Daily Menu 16
Day 10 Daily Menu 9	**Day 25** Daily Menu 14	**Day 40** Daily Menu 17	**Day 55** Daily Menu 35	**Day 70** Daily Menu 46	**Day 85** Daily Menu 51
Day 11 Daily Menu 10	**Day 26** Daily Menu 17	**Day 41** Daily Menu 27	**Day 56** Daily Menu 36	**Day 71** Daily Menu 47	**Day 86** Daily Menu 52
Day 12 Daily Menu 11	**Day 27** Daily Menu 14	**Day 42** Daily Menu 18	**Day 57** Daily Menu 37	**Day 72** Daily Menu 48	**Day 87** Daily Menu 33
Day 13 Daily Menu 12	**Day 28** Daily Menu 18	**Day 43** Daily Menu 24	**Day 58** Daily Menu 20	**Day 73** Daily Menu 44	**Day 88** Daily Menu 14
Day 14 Daily Menu 13	**Day 29** Daily Menu 19	**Day 44** Daily Menu 24	**Day 59** Daily Menu 38	**Day 74** Daily Menu 49	**Day 89** Daily Menu 14
Day 15 Daily Menu 14	**Day 30** Daily Menu 20	**Day 45** Daily Menu 28	**Day 60** Daily Menu 39	**Day 75** Daily Menu 50	**Day 90** Daily Menu 16

CPSIA information can be obtained at www.ICGtesting.com
Printed in the USA
LVOW02s2150180414

382363LV00002B/2/P